ULTRASAFE

A Guide To Safer Rock Climbing

George B. Allen

First Edition

PP Preventive Press LLC

Highlands Ranch, Colorado

ULTRASAFE
A Guide To Safer Rock Climbing
By George B. Allen

Published by:
PP Preventive Press LLC
2343 W. Hyacinth Rd.
Highlands Ranch, CO 80129

Copyright © 2001 by   PP Preventive Press LLC
2343 W. Hyacinth Rd.
Highlands Ranch, CO 80129
U.S.A.

First Printing: January 2002
Printed in the United States of America

Allen, George B.
ULTRASAFE— *A Guide To Safer Rock Climbing*
George B. Allen—1st ed.

Includes bibliographic references and index.
Library of Congress Control Number: 2001117926
ISBN 0-9669160-1-8

ACKNOWLEDGMENTS

The author's interest in enhanced climbing safety started with the pointed lessons of climbing mentors. These masters shared their secrets and alerted me to the importance of detail and safety in climbing.

Carl Braun, climber, friend, pilot, and former US Navy safety officer, provided important editorial comments.

Benjamin Hummel designed the cover. Mr. Hummel reserves all rights to the design except those conveyed to Preventive Press LLC.

The author made all final editorial and stylistic decisions.

WARNING – DISCLAIMER

Climbing is an inherently dangerous sport. No equipment, instruction guide, climbing protocol, or personal guide can eliminate all of the risks in climbing. Your decision to climb demonstrates your acceptance of the risk of serious injury or death. This book is not an inducement to climb. The book is owned by Preventive Press LLC (PP LLC), a Colorado Limited Liability Company. PP LLC makes no warranties that this instruction book is merchantable, that it provides accurate and reliable information or that the book is suitable for any specific purpose. PP LLC assumes no liability for the acts of those who consult this book.

If you wish to reduce your risk in climbing, always use a personal, certified, guide. If you do not wish to assume any risk, do not rock climb.

Ultrasafe is intended for climbers who are already skilled in basic rockcraft. It is not intended to be used as a basic climbing instruction manual, but rather as a supplement to other books and to personal instruction.

This book is designed to familiarize individuals with equipment use, protocols, hazard identification, and thought processes that enhance rock climbing safety. It is not a substitute for intensive, hands-on training by a professional climbing guide or for personally assuming the risks inherent in learning to climb. To be a competent climber requires 500 to 1000 days of leading in various areas, on various routes. Do not be fooled; athletic ability is not the same as climbing competence.

The concepts discussed in this book are specifically not intended to apply to ice climbing or mountaineering, as these sports assume an even higher level of risk.

It is not the intent of the author to review all of the material pertinent to the subject. Rather, the guide is intended to outline and organize major aspects of climbing safety. You are urged to consult original sources, including books, periodicals, the Internet, and professional guides to refine your understanding of rock climbing safety. For specific sources, see the Bibliography at the end of the book.

The stories enclosed in boxes are fiction and are not based on real people or events.

If you do not wish to be bound by the above, you may return this book at any time to the publisher, distributor, or bookseller for a full refund. The publisher, PP LLC, will make direct reimbursements and will reimburse all wholesalers or retailers.

TABLE OF CONTENTS

It is the sides of the mountain that sustain life, not the top.
    Robert Pirsig

INTRODUCTION

Why Climb?

Different people climb for different reasons: to face their fear; to enjoy gymnastic expression; as another outlet for interest in the outdoors; for adventure; or for the physical challenge. Some people climb simply to impress others with their bravery.

Few climb to expose themselves to added risk. This book has little to offer those who want more risk exposure, because the idea here is to explain how to reduce the risks inherent in climbing.

Who Climbs?

Thirty years ago the typical American climber came to climbing after apprenticeships in other outdoor pursuits like hiking and peak bagging. Most progressed from diverse outdoor experiences to status as rock climbers. Mentors guided the transition to competence.

Starting in the early 1990s climbing gyms blossomed. The gyms attracted a larger audience to rock climbing—the total number of climbers in the US has grown from thousands in the 1960s to numbering in the millions of people today (Ditmer, 2001). Lost to this new generation is the opportunity to apprentice with a mentor—there simply are not enough of them.

Climbers in the prior generation knew that climbing is both sport and craft. The "sport" side involves the pure gymnastic moves, and the "craft" portion of climbing involves everything else: gear, leading, route-finding, etiquette, natural history, and using sound judgment. People now starting in climbing have little chance to develop the craft side of the discipline because they cannot buy sufficient instruction time with a guide, and there are insufficient numbers of "journeymen" climbers available to serve as mentors in the way that benefited prior generations of climbers.

How do I know this? Because a good portion of the people I see and meet at crags do not know how to route find, analyze hazards, place gear, set anchors, or exercise good climbing judgment.

What is the Motive for Writing this Book?

My climbing career spans about 28 years and some 2000 days on the rock. During that period, about 20 friends and acquaintances died in adventure sports. In 2000, at least four climbers died on local Denver crags. By and large, these people were young – under 40.

Climbing is a great sport and a great way of life, but it need not be a way of death. I see a clear need for a climbing text that ignores discussion of gymnastics and ability and emphasizes safety.

I hope that novice and intermediate climbers read this book and that the rate of accidents and deaths in rock climbing are reduced.

Who Should Read this Book?

It takes 500 or more days of rock climbing to become a "journeyman" climber. Short of spending time with these journeymen, novices expose themselves to elevated hazards while they gain competence by trial and error.

This book discusses: (1) the common rock climbing hazards, (2) enhanced methods to manage the risk, and (3) styles of thought which reduce climbing risk. The goal of the book is to give novice and intermediate climbers a guide to enhanced safety.

Ideally, by placing safety concerns first, and understanding methods to enhance safety, beginning climbers can reduce risk as they journey to competence.

Ultrasafe is intended for individuals who are taking climbing courses, for those starting out at gyms, for organizations that teach climbing, for those transitioning from gym to sport or from sport to traditional climbing, and simply those who want to enhance their climbing safety.

Ultrasafe assumes a basic knowledge of climbing: techniques, belaying, protection, leading, anchors, and rappelling. Without this basic knowledge, the reader will be lost.

What is the Relationship between Climbing Competence and Climbing well?

Climbing well, or as climbers say, "hard," means being able to lead, follow, or boulder gymnastically difficult routes. Climbing competently means effectively using equipment, judgment, and physical ability to safely ascend and descend rock. A person who fluidly leads 5.11s may be incompetent, but climb well. A seasoned climber may be limited to routes 5.8 or easier and be competent at that level, but, by today's standards, he does not climb well. To be competent, one must be safe and in control at the desired level of difficulty.

There are four stages of competence:
1. Unconscious incompetence—the person who is incompetent and does not know it.
2. Unconscious competence—the person who is competent, but does not know it.
3. Conscious incompetence—the person who is incompetent, knows it, but is indifferent to his incompetence.
4. Conscious competence—the person who is competent and knows it.

To enhance climbing safety, *Ultrasafe* sets out to: (a) encourage the unconsciously incompetent to realize they are unsafe and to show them how to be safer; (b) encourage the unconsciously competent to move to a higher level of climbing safety through self-awareness; and (c) cause the consciously incompetent to repent and embrace safety as their credo.

Those who are consciously competent know what they are doing, but they still may benefit from a few of the *Wizard Tips* in *Ultrasafe.*

What Makes Climbing Dangerous?
There is no way to eliminate risk from rock climbing. Like scuba diving, parachuting, and space exploration, climbing is an endeavor with constant exposure to a uniformly dangerous field—gravity. If you are not holding onto the rock,

10

standing on a secure platform or hold, tied in, or safely descending, you are falling.

Because of the fall exposure, climbers can almost never let down their guard – they must always be mindful of the risk.

What are the Hazards that cause Accidental Death and Injury in Climbing?

There are three major classes or risk-types in climbing: the risk of the climber falling, the risk of something falling on the climber, and the risk caused by other environmental factors.

The American Alpine Club's annual report, *Accidents in North American Mountaineering* (Williamson, 2000), establishes that the majority of accidents occur on rock, during the ascent, and because of a slip or fall. The report concludes that climbing un-roped and exceeding one's abilities are the principal contributory causes of accidents. Poor preparation and poor-to-no climbing protection are the third and fourth most significant contributory factors to climbing accidents.

These findings suggest that poor preparation and poor judgment are the leading causes of climbing accidents.

Ultrasafe describes the risk of accidental death or injury encountered in every facet of climbing and the book discusses ways to reduce risks in climbing.

Doesn't Sport Climbing Reduce the Risk and the Incidence of Accidents?

Sport climbing reduces some of the risks of some accidents common to traditional climbing, but it appears to have increased exposure to other types of risk. In and of itself, sport climbing may be no safer than traditional climbing. Allow me to explain why.

By relying on 3/8"and 5/8" bolts for lead protection and anchors, sport climbing virtually eliminated the risk of protection failure and anchor failure.

In comparison to traditional climbing, the enhanced risk in sport climbing comes from greater exposure to:
- ❑ Falling out of otherwise sound anchors
- ❑ Being dropped during lowering
- ❑ Rappelling off the end of ropes
- ❑ Being mistakenly untied due to constantly tying-in and untying
- ❑ Ground fall because sport climbs mostly start at the ground or on ledges

The tying-untying risk means it is more likely that you will leave the belay chain because you were unsecured. The fact that sport climbs mostly start near the ground means any long fall is more likely to result in contact and injury, as opposed to traditional climbs, which progressively move up a wall and away from the impacting ground.

Isn't it just Novices who have Accidents?
No, accidental injury and death rates are a function of the severity of a hazard—the extent to which a hazard can cause injury or death—times the number of times members of the community are exposed to the risk(s). For perspective, consider the occurrence rate of accidents in commercial aviation: the likelihood of any one flight having an accident is very low, but the total probability of aircraft accidents increases

with the increasing number of flights. Clearly, competent climbers who climb a lot have an enhanced probability of having an accident compared to those who climb very little—not because they are inherently careless, but because they have frequent hazard exposure.

That is the statistical side of accident risk, but is there a root cause to competent climbers having accidents? Maybe. Industrial accident studies show new workers have an early peak in accidents prior to becoming competent in their jobs, a steady decline in accidents after they become competent, and a second peak in accidents some five years after they start their jobs.

The cause of the second peak in accidents? Complacency. Competent people loose their edge, they become bored, their level of competence effectively slips, and they have accidents.

Is there a Way to make Climbing Safer?
Climbing accident rates will decrease when the climbing community places safety ahead of performance, socializing, and naked risk-taking. This book illustrates how climbers can identify and reduce hazards in all facets of climbing.

Applying Industrial Safety to Rock Climbing
Safety professionals and industry use numerous protocols like safety plans, job-hazard analysis, training, accident investigation, and accident-rate analysis to control risks and reduce hazards. As an unregulated, loose-knit sport, climbers—thankfully—do not have the same constraints. After all, the great virtue of climbing is the expression of personal freedom, and we all know, more rules equal less freedom.

There are, however, two industrial safety concepts that climbers can adapt to their advantage—the *safety culture* and the concept of *single-point failure*. A safety culture has all players on a team making safety the highest priority; it requires players to know relevant safety issues; and it allows any one member of a team to halt an activity they deem unsafe.

Whereas the *safety culture* pertains to how people think and behave, the concept of *single-point failure* pertains to the integrity of climbing-safety systems. If the failure of any one component of a system leads the failure of the whole engineering system, then that component is a *single-failure point*. Climber's must learn to recognize *single-failure points* and to eliminate them by back-ups whenever possible. This means that you should never rappel off of a single sling or anchor into a single nut. The Climbing Safety Chapter explores, in detail, how to eliminate *single-failure points*.

Don't Safety Considerations take away from the Enjoyment of Climbing?

In the short term, putting safety first is likely to detract from socializing, spontaneity, and climbing performance. However, safer climbing enhances the chance of having a long, productive life. Furthermore, once you learn how to climb with the utmost safety, you may find your confidence built because you are less fearful of accidents. More confident climbers climb more difficult routes.

14

Adventure is just bad planning.
Roald Amundsen (1872-1928)

PREPARATION

Introduction
Being *Ultrasafe* depends on your training, experience, equipment, attitude, ability, partners, good luck, and preparation. Preparation here refers to the information you gather and analyze along with the hardware and software you choose to take.

One of the unique aspects of climbing is that resourcefulness can and does overcome many deficiencies in preparation, specifically for lack of gear. The climber with a standard rack encounters unexpected offwidths, but makes do with inventive small nut placements. Summer climbers who forgot rain gear find shelter in a boulder field. Retreating climbers manage to use tied knots as chock placements to enhance a marginal anchor.

There is no substitute for resourcefulness in climbing, but good preparation goes a long way toward reducing the risk inherent in not being prepared for foreseeable conditions.

Many climbers shortchange preparation when they step out to local crags for the day or plan a road trip—this is a mistake because being prepared enhances climbing safety.

Climate and Weather
Climate and weather play critical roles in climbing safety. Climate is the prevailing weather in an area, and weather

comprises the daily conditions. If you do not start your climbing career with an interest in meteorology, you should adopt an interest promptly. Climbing started as an exploration of the natural environment; so climbers traditionally had a natural affinity for weather observation — and many are quite good at it.

Climate exercises important controls over rock characteristics and environmental hazards: jungles have poisonous snakes; dry climates often have coarse rock; alpine environments create loose rocks. Weather affects climbing safety in that it controls daily changes in rock conditions and it can cause substantial harm or death for the unprepared climber.

To constrain the risks caused by adverse weather, the climber needs to understand climate, regional weather, seasonal weather, local weather, and immediate forecasts. Equipped with weather studies, the climber can make the best decision as to what equipment, clothes, food, and drink to bring on the pending adventure.

Discussing meteorology is beyond the scope of this book, but suffice it to say that the further the climber travels from his or her home the more he or she should study the climate, weather patterns, trends, and forecasts. Successful climbers rely heavily on understanding weather patterns to take advantage of the best window of weather.

Like never before, the Internet allows climbers to study voluminous data with little effort to unearth it. Through study and observation, you may find your forecasts more reliable for climbing than those of meteorologists. For example, mountaineers know well that massifs, groups of mountains, create their own local weather—weather not routinely reported by forecasters.

In the conterminous US, by far the most stable weather window occurs in early fall—generally between September 5 and October 1. This is the safest time to climb—the only drawback being that the days are shorter, and evening bivouacs are colder than in summer. Obviously, this window varies with region—bigger in the Southwest and smaller in New England. In the Southwest this window extends well into November. Unlike the rest of the country, the Southwest enjoys a similarly stable period in March and April.

In contrast, the most volatile weather comes in early winter, usually late December to early January, in the spring, and during the summer monsoon season. Of these, monsoonal summer is perhaps the most dangerous season because of its dramatic lightning storms.

The remainder of the year, early summer, late fall, late summer, offer less stable weather, but many fine days.

Lightning is the big Kahuna of weather dangers. The best strategy to avoid this hazard is to learn when lightning storms form in the region where you will climb and to be off the routes during those periods. If you are stuck, try your best to be away from high points, wet cracks, caves, trees and metal—fat chance if you are stuck. Remember, lightning's proximity is measured by the time between the lightning strike and its thunder. Three rules of thumb: (a) if the time gap between the lightning and thunder is less than 30 seconds, it's time to take cover, (b) every five seconds between the lightning and thunder marks one mile of distance from the observer, and (c) the leading and trailing edge of storms pose the greatest lightning risks. For more, see the National Lightning Safety Institute's Website.

Training

In climbing, training traditionally refers to physical training. Safety training is called climbing instruction.

Effective physical and mental conditioning prove over and over again to overcome deficiencies in other types of preparation. Consider that some climbers have confidently free-soloed climbs that lesser, *uber*-equipped parties failed to ascend.

Physical training, however, will not be discussed here. There are many available books that emphasize training (see Bibliography). More importantly, accident analysis shows that physical deficiencies are most often secondary contributors to accidents. The primary contributors are poor preparedness, bad safety techniques, and bad judgment—major subject areas of this book.

As to instruction, all new climbers must receive it—whether through competent mentors or in formal classes, every climber needs instruction to learn the basics. Take note, however, there are problems associated with receiving instruction:

- ❑ Since there are no uniform climbing standards or required certification for guides, you can never be sure if you are learning the right things.
- ❑ There are many people who now start out in climbing gyms. Addressed in the third section

of this book, *Climbing Safety*, some gyms foster some practices which are not suitable for traditional or sport climbing in the natural environment. One-thousand days of gym time does not a climber make.

❑ Climbing is as much trade as it is a sport—to be minimally competent you must climb independently for 500 to 1000 days in diverse outdoor areas.

❑ Relying too much on guiding can slow your progress. Only by climbing and progressively challenging yourself will you achieve mastery. If you pay someone to lead and make decisions, you may never develop climbing judgment.

Having said all that, the traditional route toward competence includes following *bona fide* guides for five to ten days, an intensive "outdoor experience" course for a month or so, following an experienced leader for 50 or so days, reading a variety of instructional guides, and climbing with partners on progressively challenging climbs. Obviously, working with a mentor from the outset can supersede the need for any of the first three phases.

Clothes

Clothes contribute importantly to climbing safety in that they allow the climber to handle varied weather. Inexperienced climbers assume that the conditions on their porch will prevail throughout the day. Lacking the right clothes enhances the risk of dehydration, heat exhaustion, heat stroke, hypothermia, and frostbite. Insidiously, weather-related medical conditions and less severe discomfort contribute to poor decisions, a major contributor to climbing accidents.

For almost 100 years wool was the gold standard for climbers. Since the invention of nylon during World War II, climbers have been afforded a great variety of synthetics, most of which are far handier than wool. Wool socks are still useful for cold days.

The most common problem arises from not having the right kind or amount of extra clothes. To avoid problems with body temperature, consider the following:

- The heavier the piece of clothing, the less likely you will be inclined to take it with you on a climb.

- Climbers get the most warmth for the least weight from warm socks, a stocking hat, and a wind shell.

- Spring, summer, winter, or fall, the single best accessory is a stocking cap. The traditional Scottish head covering, the balaclava looks funky, but it is well suited to climbing because you can clip the chin portion to a carabiner to avoid loss when not in use. Two-ounce poly-pro balaclavas are wonderful, all-season accessories for your rucksack.

- A hat is essential to protect against too much sun. Not having one enhances your exposure to sunburn, sunstroke, heat exhaustion, and dehydration. The best hats have small loops so they can be attached to harnesses, bandolier slings, or packs while the climber is active.

❑ The single most versatile body covering is the wind shell. While not waterproof, a light, hooded, wind shirt is essential. These make you comfortable in the face of increasing wind or a less than ten-degree temperature drop. Importantly, they are very light and less likely to be left in the rucksack. For wet weather or wet climates, it is better to bring along a waterproof shell.

❑ The early days of spring inspire premature breakouts of shorts. Shorts are fine, but bring pants or wind-pant coverings for changes in the weather.

❑ For climbs with potentially extreme weather, the climber must judge how many extra clothes to bring. Typical accessories are: pile coats and pants, mittens, and waterproof shells.

❑ In the spring and fall, start off with long-sleeve shirts and long pants. If you are too hot, roll 'em up.

Wizard Tip—If you have worn-out extra clothes, ropes, and shoes, consider stashing some in your car for emergencies. Partners often show up without necessary clothes. Extra chalk bags, climbing shoes, rope and harness sometimes are useful too. Be careful with the used rope and harness.

Photo 1. Standard garb for temperate days includes balaclava, windshirt, water bottle, sunglasses and hat.

Shoes

Climbers rely on two types of shoes—approach and climbing. Inappropriate approach shoes—tennis shoes, dress shoes, adventure sandals—put a climber at risk of fall, injury and/or twisted ankles. Adventure sandals are risky because they leave feet open to rock-fall and possibly being impaled on sticks. Also, upturned toes can cause you to trip.

Nowadays, there is no shortage of lightweight approach options. Climbers can choose from $100+ shoes at climbing shops, mid-priced low-tops at retail chains, or they can even buy functional shoes at discount retailers.

The important options in shoes are low-tops versus high-tops and aggressive soles versus "sticky soles." Some people feel that high-tops provide more ankle support. When adopting this argument, climbers need to remember that low-tops are more likely to ride up climbs than are high high-tops; that supportive high-top is no help at all if it is left at the base of most climbs. The aggressive sole versus "sticky" sole argument is less vexing. Aggressive soles work well in mud and dirt. "Sticky" soles rule on dry slabs and sandstone terrain.

Photo 2. Open-toed shoes are dangerous for approaches.

> *Wizard Tip*— Always tie or clip your shoes together when they are not is use. Unpaired shoes uncannily run away from each other.

The fit and the appropriateness of the shoe to the climb are the major safety considerations involved in choosing a climbing shoe. As for fit, whoever tells you that climbing shoes should be so tight that they hurt is wrong. Unless you seek ultimate performance, climbing shoes should be comfortable and they should feel familiar before you head out on a perilous journey.

As for appropriateness of the shoe to the climb, slippers work great on most sport routes, but as the routes get longer and cracks rule over face holds, climbers will want sturdier shoes with laces and high tops. Few things distract more than tight-fitting slippers on multi-pitch crack climbs.

Personal Protection Equipment

Harnesses

First-string climbers in the 1970s sported swami belts — one-inch or two-inch tubular webbing wrapped around the waist. These things are highly macho — they discourage falling and hanging — but are equally uncomfortable and unsafe. Thankfully, standards have changed, and climbers now routinely wear sewn harnesses with leg loops.

The buckle is the problem with the harness. Climbers forget to buckle, or after relieving themselves, forget to properly rebuckle. This lapse has caused a number of serious accidents and deaths.

There are two ways to reduce the chance of falling out of an unbuckled harness: (a) Use a harness made with a buckle that is permanently bound. The buckle loosens and tightens, but cannot be undone; or (b) Wear a back-up swami belt. The back-up swami goes under your harness and consists of one-inch tubular webbing wrapped three or four times around your waist and tied with a water knot. This device does not completely eliminate the chance of falling out of the harness, but if used correctly and consistently, it may catch you the one time you forget to buckle. The only safe way to use the backup is to always tie into all of the waist loops. If you miss one, the rest will cinch up tightly in a serious fall and could cause internal damage. Even if you do correctly tie through the back-up harness, in a serious fall you could have internal organ, back, or spine injuries. The trade-off is that you may live with those injuries, whereas you are unlikely to live with the injuries resulting from a free fall out of your harness. Make no mistake, deciding to use a back-up swami exposes you to an added danger; hence doing so is an imperfect solution. If your stomach muscles are weak, the swami may pose a higher hazard and should not be used.

The true *Safety Buffalo* will wear a chest harness with the sit harness, but no one, save children and cavers, wear these in the US. Children's harnesses are the exception with full-body setup that includes a chest component.

Harnesses can fail you in more ways than one. Whereas most contemporary harnesses have fixed-width leg loops, some less expensive harnesses come with a strap that goes under the seat and is held in place by cinches that tighten to the front. If the strap is not set tightly enough, it may cause a groin injury when you fall. To avoid these injuries, make sure all harnesses fit snugly—especially in the legs. If you participate in winter climbing as well as fair-weather climbing, you will need adjustable leg loops or more than one harness.

Glasses

Note to the visually impaired—for a price, you can buy prescription lenses and frames that meet the ANSI (engineered to prevent injury) standard. These will not shatter or damage your eyes. Safety goggles are even better, but they look funky and no one wears them.

Helmets

Chief Yosemite Rescue Ranger, John Dill writes, "...a helmet doesn't make you invincible. What goes on inside your head is more important than what you wear on it."

That been said there are some rock climbing occasions when helmets are nearly essential:
- For the new leader
- In known rock-fall zones
- On popular climbs where other parties loom above
- When the climber plans to climb at his or her limit and is likely to fall
- On climbs where leader falls will invariably lead to climber-rock impact
- For children

If you can develop the habit of always wearing a helmet, that is all the better. One detriment to helmets is that they make you hotter. While fine in the cool seasons, this could make a climber more susceptible to heat exhaustion and heat prostration in summer.

As a final consideration, note that if you become accustomed to a helmet and then stop using it, you will find yourself unpleasantly tapping your naked head against the rock because your mind still anticipates that extra head shell.

Ropes

Deciding which rope to own and which one to use is a difficult decision. Ropes are the single most expensive item in most climbers' repertoire, and few people have more than one in active service at any one time. There are three main options:

- ❑ The traditional 11 mm
- ❑ The various sub-11 mm's—the 10.5 mm, 10 mm, and 9.8 mm single-line ropes
- ❑ The double 9-mm or double 8.8-mm setup

The advantage of the 11 mm is that it is somewhat less likely to cut over an edge, easier to hold a fall, and somewhat more durable. The enhanced durability makes it more likely to last longer than smaller diameter ropes. The disadvantages are its weight, its bulkiness in a coil, and its enhanced resistance to flowing through some belay devices. As a counterweight to the belay-device flow problem, 11 mm's often "break" more readily in a belay—this means they are better at catching leader falls. Finally, 11-mm ropes run more slowly through rappel devices, an advantage to "plus-sized" climbers, and a disadvantage to the petite.

The advantages of the sub-11 mm ropes are that they are lighter and easier to coil and belay. The lighter weight is important for those who emphasize climbing performance. The greatest disadvantage of a sub-11mm rope is that it is more likely to be cut through than is an 11 mm or a double-rope system. Also, the sub-11 mm's require more hand strength to catch a fall and to rappel than do larger diameter ropes. Lighter weight climbers may find this to be an advantage on rappel. The better flow characteristics save petite climbers from having to "pump" the rope through rappel devices.

Photo 3. Rope choices (L to R): 11 mm, 10.5 mm, 9 mm, 9 mm static line.

The advantages of the double-rope system are more apparent to mountaineers than to rock climbers: The system provides a team with two ropes at all times; two ropes are almost never cut simultaneously; and the double-rope system reduces rope drag on climbs that traverse back and forth. A fourth advantage is that, used properly, double ropes can eliminate or reduce the likelihood of lead falls when the leader is clipping a higher piece of protection. The reduced risk comes from the fact that one rope can stay static, at the leader's waist, while the second rope is pulled over his head for a higher clip-in. If the leader falls during the clip, instead of falling until all the slack on the top rope is taken up, he only falls through the slack line at his waist.

The disadvantages of the double-rope system are that they are more difficult to use in belay devices than single ropes;

they are more likely to form tangles; they require more rope management; and they do not allow the use of passive belay devices like Grigris. Also, a double 9-mm or 8.8-mm rappel is very fast for climbers who weigh more than 150 lbs. The lesser resistance requires more hand strength. If a climber is profoundly fatigued, the extra strength needed could present a threat to his or her safety.

Which rope system is safest depends on the individual climb and the climbing team. In general, an 11-mm rope is safest for routine traditional climbs, but long climbs, ones that emphasize speed as a safety factor, may be best served by a sub-11 mm rope.

Sub-11 mm ropes are well suited to sport climbs which do not routinely have rope-cut hazards. Limestone presents perhaps the worst sport climbing rope-cut hazard, so an 11-mm rope may provide an enhanced level of security on some limestone crags.

Long traditional climbs, and some long sport climbs are well served by double ropes. These long climbs often require two ropes for the descent or for the possibility of retreat. Double ropes also assure that if one rope is cut, the second one may permit self-rescue. Finally, long climbs often include non-linear pitches, and the double-rope technique allows the proficient leader to substantially reduce rope drag, thereby assuring long leads. Making full-length leads is often faster than splitting up a climb into short leads. Climbing faster often enhances a team's safety because shorter climbing time concentrates strength and reduces the team's exposure to bad weather.

If a climber puts safety first, and he or she can only afford one rope, the 11 mm may be the best choice. It is a compromise between the least resistant to cut failure, the double-rope configuration, and the configuration most susceptible to cut failure—the sub-11 mm ropes. The main safety shortcoming of the 11 mm is its enhanced resistance to flowing through belay devices. New devices, those without wear grooves, pose the worst problem. You can either spend some off-rock time running the rope through the device to set a groove, or live with the resistance until a wear groove forms.

Both size and length matter. In the 1960s standard rope length was 120′. By the early 1970s standard rope length was 150′. Toward the latter part of the 1970, the European standard, 50 meters, or 165′ became *de rigueur*. And we get longer and longer. By the mid-1990s many in the climbing community accepted the 60-meter or, 200′ ropes as the norm.

Clearly, 120′ and 150′ ropes serve a very limited role—top-roping. One-hundred-and-sixty-five-foot ropes serve well on the vast majority of traditional climbs in the Western Hemisphere. Sport climbs are another story. Increasingly, sport climbs are set to 100′ heights, thereby requiring 200′ ropes for single-rope descents. The lack of 200′ ropes has contributed to a number of serious accidents and deaths as climbers unwittingly lower off 100′-high anchors. When the end of the rope meets the belay device and passes through, the climber falls some 5′ or more to the ground or a ledge.

For this reason, the dedicated sport climber should buy a 60-meter rope. Those climbers who only climb traditional climbs may be well served by 165′ ropes. Those who climb both sport and traditional should be mindful of the height of all pitches they plan to lower or rap off.

There is one last consideration to rue in rope selection—the second rope. Someone who frequently climbs multi-pitch climbs will need a second rope. There are three basic options:

- The 11-mm full-diameter rope
- The sub-11 mm ropes; 10.5 mm, 10 mm, 9 mm, or 8.8 mm
- The static line, generally a 9-mm diameter

As stated for the discussion of lead ropes, 11-mm ropes have the advantage being less subject to complete cuts, eminently suitable to take over for a damaged lead rope, and helpful in providing slower rappel descents for heavier climbers. The disadvantage to 11-mm second ropes is they are HEAVY, more prone to being stuck upon pulling a rappel, and they are more difficult for lighter climbers to use.

The advantage of sub-11 mm ropes is that they are light, they handle more easily than 11-mm ropes, and they pull through descent rings more easily than 11-mm ropes. Also, they can be used as a lead rope if the lead rope is damaged. The principal shortcoming with sub-11 mm second ropes is that they are more susceptible to complete rope cuts than are 11-mm ropes. Another shortcoming is that they stretch more than 11-mm ropes, and this is a slight disadvantage if the rope is used to haul gear or a haul sack.

The introduction of static line ropes for descents is a recent phenomenon in American climbing. Static lines do not stretch. Since they are not dynamic, they CANNOT be used for lead belays. They subject the falling leader to dangerous levels of stress. The advantage of these lines is that they are more resistant to wear and cuts, and without stretch, they make hauling easier. Like sub-11 mm dynamic ropes, these 9-mm ropes are less likely to snag during rope retrievals than are 11-mm ropes.

For double-rope descents on moderate climbs, a dynamic 9-mm rope offers the best compromise of weight and durability with minor sacrifice to safety. The static rope may offer the greatest compromise to security, because it cannot be used in a self-rescue as a lead rope—effectively leaving the party without a back-up lead rope. In contrast the single-length, dynamic 9-mm rope can be doubled and used as an 80′ double 9-mm rope in a pinch.

> *Wizard Tip*—If you use a 9-mm rope tied to a 10.5- or 11-mm for a double-rope rappel, pull the thinner rope through the descent rings or chains when facing cracks or blocks that threaten to catch a flying rope end. The thinner rope is less likely to jam in a crack on its free-fall back to you. This scenario requires the team to "pull thick to get thin."
>
> Before you pull the ropes, double check to make sure the rope that will pull through the descent rings is free of knots.

In summary, deciding which rope to buy or pack bears importantly on safety, and the climber must carefully analyze his or her needs.

Belay Devices

There are two types of belay devices, active and passive. Active devices require the belayer to always grip the rope to hold a fall. These devices have one or two holes through which you pull the rope. The original active device was the sticht plate, a two-holed unit designed for single rope, double ropes, or rappelling. More recently, tube units, like "ATCs" have become more popular.

Photo 4. Belay and rappel devices (L to R): Sticht-type, Grigri, Figure-eight.

Passive devices, like Grigris appeared on the climbing scene in the 1990s. Grigris have a cam, which engages when the paid-out end is tugged. These devices are ideal for sport climbing. The manufacturer does not recommend these devices for belaying on traditional belays. These devices are highly advantageous on climbs where the leader is taking a long time, because they do not require the same high level of attention as do sticht-type devices. Note that Grigris will not pay out when a desperate leader yanks the rope; so you must read the instructions and practice extensively before using them.

Rappel Devices

There are four well-established rappel devices:
1. Figure-eight device
2. "Sticht"-type two-hole device
3. Double carabiner
4. Munter hitch

Every climber needs to learn how to set-up and use double-carabiner rappels and munter hitches. These are conventional self-rescue rappels if you find yourself short of gear. The double carabiner rappel is set up using one locking biner and four non-locking biners, or using six non-locking biners. The safety drawback of this system is that it requires sufficient strength to pull double ropes up into the center of two biners. This may be hard if a climber is tired, hot, or cold. Consequently, relying on this technique may cause an accident. Also, this technique takes quite a bit more time to set up than using an eight or a plate, and time lost can diminish a safety margin. To its advantage, the double-carabiner brake is slow on the descent; so it does not require a tired climber to have a lot of hand strength.

The munter hitch is formed by making a loop, a simple crossing of the rope, and then folding the loop back on itself. Many people are flustered by the folding process and by their attempts to clip the two strands of rope to a locking carabiner or through two carabiners with opposed and reversed gates. This knot, like the clove-hitch, seems to take a lot of practice to master confidently. In experienced hands, the munter hitch works well for a rappel, but it is difficult to use if you are tired because it requires substantial grip. The munter hitch can also be used for a belay.

The currently preferred rappel method is the use of the tube-unit, sticht plate or one of the many variations on this two-hole device. These devices have the virtue of controlling descents with little hand strength, and of being easy to set up. These devices may contribute to serious accidents resulting from climber's failure to clip one or both of the double ropes into their locking-waist carabiners. I suspect the problem is that tired or careless climbers fail to see the actual clipping of the ropes into the carabiners. When they lean back, they are unattached and fall.

Figure-eights have the virtue of fully displaying the ropes in their course through the device and of affording the climber the satisfaction of hearing—by click—and feeling—by metal contact—the device as it seats into the locking biner at the waist.

> *Warning*—The 1970s were the heyday of the "breakbar," a small bar that clipped onto one side of a carabiner and crossed over to the other. The climber passed the double rope over the bar making a break. These are unsafe and long discredited. Leave these artifacts in the museums.

The fact that three senses may detect the climber's attachment to an eight, make these devices the least likely to cause a "failure-to-clip" accident. One drawback of the eight is that it does not provide as slow or controlled a descent as a "sticht"-type plate. This can be an important consideration for the plus-sized climber who is cleaning a sport route, because he will need more strength to hold onto an eight than if he were descending with a sticht plate.

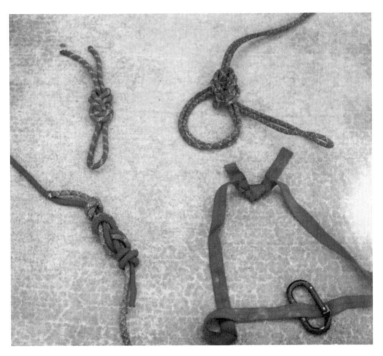

Photo 5. Essential knots (clockwise from upper left): Figure-8, bowline on a bight, water knot, and figure-eight follow-through with back-up ½-fisherman knots.

One way to add resistance to a figure-eight setup is to add a second biner at your waist clip-in and then clip it through the rope where it passes around the small hole of the two eight holes.

A new device, the SBG Belay Device, made by Omega Pacific, incorporates a figure-eight into a "sticht-type" plate. This device eliminates the need for carrying a separate belay and rappel device.

36

Self-Rescue Gear

"Newbies" advertise their status by carrying self-rescue gear—usually a pair of prussik slings—five- or six-foot long chords that may be tied onto a rope with an ascending knot. All climbers should be prepared to self-rescue, but it is unwieldy to carry 8'-loops that seldom see use. Better to carry a few shoulder-length 6-mm or 7-mm slings that can be used as needed for extension on climbs and are available in the event of an emergency. Better still, learn how to tie a hitch on a sling—a hedden knot, which can be used for ascending a rope just like a prussik knot. Learning how to make do with a standard set of gear enables the climber to climb lighter and encourages creative thinking.

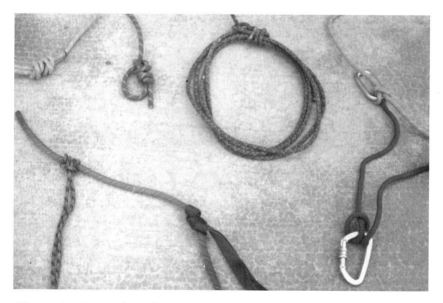

Photo 6. Secondary knots (clockwise from upper left): double fisherman, bowline with backup, bowline on coil, clove hitch, munter hitch, hedden knot, and prussik.

Climbing Hardware

The number of available hardware choices is bewildering. Carrying too little, too much, or the wrong hardware endangers a leader. Here is a basic rack that will serve most moderate climbs:

Hexes spanning 1" to 3.5"; 12 to 15 wired stoppers ranging from 1/16" to 1" diameter; 5 cams with ½" to 4" span.

Hexes have many advantages over cams:

- When used properly, hexes are more likely to resist being pulled out.
- They are better suited to multi-directional anchors than are cams.
- It is easier to judge the soundness of a hex than of a cam.
- A climber is more likely to leave a $10 hex in an emergency than to leave a $55 cam.

> *Wizard Tip*—It's not the brand or style of the biner that counts so much as how you fall on it. Note that the short axis of a biner, the span from the gate to its opposing side, is not strong when the gate is open or ajar. Biners can and do break. Never trust a single biner if its failure will cause injury or death. Use heavy-duty locking biners, double biners or double quickdraws in situations where biner failure will lead to death or serious injury.
>
> Having said that, you may assume heavier biners are sturdier, and lighter ones are more susceptible to breaking.

Cams enhance the overall safety of a lead because they can be quickly placed and go into slots where hexes don't work.

In short, a blend of hexes and cams contributes to the highest level of leader safety.

Photo 7. Standard rack, note optional cheater stick (clip).

The standard rack should be supplemented with other gear as needed—add brass nuts in face climbing and thin-crack areas; add finger size for finger cracks; 2" and 3" pieces for hand cracks, and so on.

Slings

Slings are available in a variety of diameters, lengths and connections. A standard length is about five feet. When tied or sewn it hangs over one shoulder down to about belly level. Many novices buy double- or triple-length slings because they serve them well for setting up top ropes. These long slings create a mess on the lead and should be left at home unless the climber knows that they are needed for the particular climb.

Sewn slings look neat and are stronger than tied slings, but traditional climbers should always carry an assortment of sewn and tied slings—the tied slings come in handy if you have to thread a chock stone, hole, deformed piton eye, or retreat anchors.

Even sport climbers should have two or three tied slings for retreats. A locking carabiner makes for a safer retreat, but some climbers feel that a carabiner costs too much to leave one on a climb. Absent a throw-away sling, cheap climbers may be more inclined to do something dangerous rather than leave a $5 biner—better to give yourself the option by keeping a stash of throw-away slings. If you must leave a sling to lower off, always leave at least two, and never rap off less than two substantial pieces of protection.

> *Wizard Tips*—Weight newly tied slings to tighten the knot on them. Do this by first affixing one end of the sling and then standing or jumping on the other end. To loosen a tightened sling, moisten it and use a nut tool to pry the knot open. Avoid using your teeth.
>
> For removing old slings or, in a dire emergency, for cutting your beloved rope, a small one-inch folding knife blade is invaluable. Although a larger blade would undoubtedly be more useful, they seldom make it into day or fanny packs.

Having too few slings can also diminish climbing safety. Without sufficient slings for use as protection-extension, there can be excessive rope drag, or a piece of protection could pull out. As a rule of thumb, you will need one quickdraw or shoulder-length sling, plus two biners, for each piece of gear you plan to place. You will also need a few slings and carabiners to clip into the anchor.

Stick Clips are poles that extend a climber's reach to clip bolts high off the ground or to clip out-of-reach gear on routes. The typical stick-clip has a carabiner at one end. The rope is threaded through the biner and the extended stick is thrust up to the first bolt. Using stick-clips can protect leaders from dangerous run-outs up to the first protection. Climbers can also make small, 12" to 18" "porta-stick-clips" which can be carried on climbs and used to clip out-of-reach bolts. These porta-clips pose their own hazard—a fall onto one could impale the leader or otherwise hurt him.

Gear Maintenance

Equipment suitability falls into four categories: new, stable, in need of repair, or ready to retire. Knowing when to retire or fix gear is critical to climbing safety. When you first buy gear, don't throw out the attached instructions—read them. Note especially the manufacturers recommended shelf life. This is the total number of years gear can and should be used even if—at the end of the prescribed period—it is still in good condition. Many climbers ignore the recommended shelf life for hardware, but no one should ignore these guidelines for software like harnesses and ropes. As hydrocarbon products, chemicals can imperceptibly damage ropes and harnesses, so the absence of visible damage is not a testament to the soundness of a product.

So long as gear is within its shelf life, you only need to periodically inspect it. Ropes and harnesses may continue to be used so long as they have no stains, tears, cuts, bumps, solvent exposure, or extreme abrasion. For a detailed discussion of rope wear see Damian Wear's website. For harnesses, beware of unfurling stitching. For ropes, beware of cores that are sliding through sheaths.

41

Ready For Retirement—A Story. "K" retired from a successful engineering career to dedicate himself to climbing. A mutual friend hooked us up, and I was thankful to meet another old bird. He pulled out a tattered rope that had one spot where the sheath was torn exposing the core. I balked at the sight of the rope and vowed not to do anything serious on it. Later that afternoon I was shot full of adrenaline as I top-roped a 5.11 roof in Boulder Creek, Colorado, inspired by the sight of the bleach-white rope core bulging out above me. I crossed "K" off of my "available list" after that occasion.

With hardware—biners, cams, and nuts—look out for bends, burrs and sticking. A bent nut or cam is probably ready for the scrap heap. A minor burr may be filed down. Unfurling cables on nuts and cams requires replacement of the entire cable or retiring the piece. The broken cable strand makes for a substandard piece and it can injure someone. When the plastic fitting that holds the wires together breaks, it can be replaced with "shrink tape," which is sold by electrical supply shops.

Biners and cams both stick in fixed positions when they become sandy or dirty. The grains can be removed by using degreaser and Q-tips. The final coat should be a non-stick lubricant like silicone spray. Be careful to stay away from sources of ignition while handling flammable spray lubricants. Some climbers recommend soaking cams in a pot of white gas to float off particulates—DO NOT DO THIS. A pool of white gas is dangerous and highly flammable. If it spills on you and ignites, if the filled container ignites, or if fumes ignite from a water heater or furnace, you could suffer a serious injury or death.

Used Gear

Admit it. Everyone who climbs uses secondhand gear during his or her climbing career. It is unavoidable unless you choose to replace every fixed anchor you ever encounter— something akin to carrying your own toilet in public. I have yet to meet a climber who can resist scarfing booty. So the real question is not whether or not to use secondhand gear, but what limits to put on its use. Here is an outline that can provide some guidance:

Never Accept or Use—Secondhand ropes or harnesses

Use with Great Caution—Helmets, secondhand or found slings, carabiners, and secondhand cam devices

Use after Inspection—Stoppers, hexes, and other passive hardware

Use with Abandon after Cleaning—Secondhand shoes, packs, clothes and accessories

So what is wrong with secondhand ropes and harnesses? Simply, the risk far outweighs the reward. The rope and harness are so essential to safety that no uncertainty as to their integrity is worth incurring. Factors like sun and chemical exposure cause unseen damage; you can never be sure of the history of secondhand ropes and harnesses. Besides, retailers now routinely sell new UIAA-certified ropes for $99—why be so cheap? The only exception to this rule is if you want to cut up a rope to use for slings. Nine-mm ropes are especially good for "leaver" slings.

What's wrong with secondhand helmets, slings, biners, and cams? Helmets could have exposure to chemicals that altered the plastic, or perhaps, damage from a fall could be concealed. Best to buy your own new helmet. Slings can have undetectable sun or chemical exposure, which weaken them. You may keep a few to use in situations where you need to leave a sling. But they should only be left at anchors in combination with two or three other slings that appear to be sound. Never retreat off one sling—especially not off a secondhand one. For some cheap climbers, hoarding "leaver" slings may enhance their safety because they are more inclined to back-up an anchor with slings they never paid for than they would be if they had to leave something costly. If you insist on hoarding "leaver" slings, consider inking the ends to signify to you that they are not for prime-time use.

As to unseen flaws in biners and cams? Drops, pounding, or extreme falls could all exceed the tensile strength of the unit, leaving microflaws, which, absent metallurgical tests, are not detectable. The best use for secondhand biners and cams is as back-ups or "leaver" gear. The problem with keeping gear to leave is that it often creeps into the climber's normal rack and gets used along with pedigreed gear. If you insist on keeping neutered biners, consider painting them to warn yourself against using them in critical situations.

Stoppers, hexes and other passive gear are the hardware most likely to maintain their integrity after a stress event; so they may be acceptable used gear. Inspect the booty for pound marks, shears, fractures, and broken cable strands. Reject any gear with one or more or these visible flaws. As with any gear, a climber should never rely on any one piece as "failsafe;" the core principal of *Ultrasafe* methodology is to back-up anything and everything that can be backed-up. Ultimately, secondhand hardware is best stored as "leaver" gear. Similar to secondhand slings, cheap climbers may enhance their safety by collecting "leaver" gear because they are more likely to leave it, and therefore, more likely to back-up rappel anchors.

The only danger presented by used shoes and clothes arise from bad fit, bad smell, and communicable diseases—wash stuff thoroughly and you should be OK.

Areas New to You

Climbers get all excited when they arrive at areas new to them. Don't let the excitement supersede good judgment. The safe thing to do is to start off on climbs that are a few number grades below your limit. If you are used to 5.10, start out on a 5.8 followed by a 5.9. Unless you are highly seasoned, easing into a new area is advisable because rock, grades, protection, and the degree to which climbs are sustained vary highly from area to area. Consider this:

❑ A Devil's Lake, Wisc., 5.10c is likely to be un-protected and feel remarkably as hard as a 5.11 at Owen's Gorge, Calif.

❑ The person who routinely leads 5.11 face climbs at Table Mountain, Colo., is unlikely to successfully lead a sustained, layback finger-crack on the Good Book at the Folly Cliff, 5.10d, in Yosemite Valley, Calif.

❑ If you are used to granite cracks, you may feel ill at ease by the absence of cracks to place gear on your first day on the limestone at Shelf Road, Colo.

45

Giving yourself time to adjust to new areas enhances your safety by giving you a higher degree of control than you would feel if you jumped onto climbs at your limit.

If an area involves more than a trivial approach, having a topographic map is worthwhile. The added info may well save you from getting lost or hurt.

Guidebook and Beta

Climbing books advise about types of climbs, weather, needed gear, grades, standards, and much more—all critical information for hazard analysis.

Remember though, climbing guides can be misleading and deficient:

- Topos may be inaccurate.
- All dangers may not be disclosed.
- The standards of difficulty may be higher than those familiar to you.
- Individual climbs can change over time— holds, protection, and anchors may disappear.
- Route descriptions or location plans may be misleading—causing you to start on a climb more difficult or dangerous than you had intended.

Many guides fail to encourage the greatest possible safety margin by advising climbers to carry minimally sufficient racks, and in sport areas, by failing to advise that you can enhance safety on a high percentage of sport climbs by carrying and placing nuts and cams.

Some guidebook writers deliberately sandbag readers by understating the difficulty of a climb. (Sandbagging is the failure to disclose unusual difficulties or dangers. Climbers sandbag other climbers to demonstrate their prowess or enhance their own reputation as "hardmen.")

> *Wizard Tip*—Photocopy climbing topos to bring along on multi-pitch climbs.

Guidebooks are essential safety resources, but they are no substitute for good judgment.

Beta—informal advice—warrants a higher level of suspicion than afforded by guidebooks. Many climbers give beta in good faith, but some don't. Motivations for giving bad beta are the desire to sandbag and the desire to steer parties away from proprietary routes. When given beta, consider the source before you act on it.

International Trips

International trips, especially those to less-developed countries, require a higher level of preparedness than do domestic exploits. Since this book targets novices and intermediates, and international climbing is more for expert climbers, I will not detail the added preparation needed for international climbing, but here is an overview.

Added safety considerations for foreign travel include additional health risks, the fact that rescues and emergency medical care may be unavailable or poor, and climbing customs differ. For example, if Mexico's El Potrero Chico sounds like a south-of-the-border version of Shelf Road, Colo.—beware, it is not. Many climbs are long; there is no

47

established rescue team; there are no quality emergency services; there is abundant loose rock; and you might fall on a sword-like agave cactus!

> *Wizard Tip—*"Hardmen" blanch at the idea of using a personal guide. But hiring a guide in a foreign country, or at a formidable domestic area, if only for a day or so, can pay great dividends in providing area knowledge and enhancing climber safety.

Notification

Notify someone about your climbing plans. Climbers routinely fail to tell responsible parties where they are going, what they are doing, and when they plan to be back.

Serious injuries are difficult to evacuate. A rapid rescue can make the difference between a fatality and a short-term setback.

Obviously, if you are going to a place with many other climbers, the need to tell others your whereabouts is lessened. The more remote the climbing, the greater the need to inform others.

When you tell someone about your expected return, make sure you give yourself some leeway — "I'll be back between 4 PM and 6:30 PM."

First Aid and Rescue

Truth is if you, your companion, or others are too seriously hurt to get themselves to help, the best plan is to get help to you as soon as possible. Typically, the fastest way to get help in the US is to use a cell phone.

Absent a cell phone, climbers routinely stabilize the victim and go for help as expeditiously as possible. Note: injured people are often in shock and cannot be expected to act rationally. An injured climber must be secured and stabilized before you leave him. He may try to move himself and cause further injury or death.

Understanding these likely accident scenarios, the best first-aid and rescue preparation consists of taking first-aid courses, carrying sufficient first-aid gear, climbing in areas with others nearby, and keeping a cell phone at hand.

Rescue Insurance

Not long ago political jurisdictions such as counties and parks covered the costs of all rescues. Increased costs and liability have caused some political entities to limit their rescue services, or to force accident victims to pay for the service.

Each jurisdiction has its own policy. Here are some considerations to take into account when weighing the need for rescue insurance:

- In general, National Parks in the US do not charge for rescues. Denali National Park covers its rescue costs by charging for climbing permits. This user-fee system may be the trend of the future.
- County rescue teams usually do not charge for rescue, but different states allow them to charge, at their discretion. Usually, the county authorities exercise their discretion to charge if the victim is "negligent" in contributing to the

accident. If you want to know more, talk to a lawyer.

❑ County Rescue teams serve on state park rescues.

❑ Colorado offers rescue insurance for all those who buy hunting or fishing licenses. Remarkably, climbers can buy into the same insurance pool with the State Department of Parks when they purchase a "hiking insurance card" for $1.

❑ The American Alpine Club (http://www.americanalpineclub.org) provides rescue coverage to all of its members. Annual membership costs $75. Check liability limitations.

❑ Some private insurance companies have recently offered both rescue and accident insurance specifically for climbers.

❑ For those climbing overseas, the British Alpine Club is a good source of insurance.

❑ European rescue teams routinely charge for rescues, so insurance is *de rigueur.*

Truthfully, few casual climbers buy any coverage, but the diehard *Safety Buffalo* will want to study this issue as he enters varied political jurisdictions. A call to the presiding park or county officials should yield an answer.

Check Lists

Extensive preparation does little good if you forget something. Anyone who climbs for very long has the deflating experience of showing up to crag *sans* shoes, harness, rope, hardware, guidebook, hat, lunch, sunscreen, windshirt ...whatever! The remedy for this is to go through your gear just before you leave for the day or for the road trip. Developing this habit will save a climber untold grief in his or her climbing career. Some people check by list, others just visually inspect and use a mental checklist to assure the bare essentials are present and accounted.

It is more difficult to impose the same check standard on a partner, but they are just as likely as you are to forget something. I explain to partners that from time to time I have: climbed in a "swiss seat" harness; climbed barefoot; nearly froze to death because I forgot my windshirt; starved without my energy bar; and parched without anything to drink. Once I tell these stories a few times, most people accept a little quizzing, "Rope, harness shoes? ...Hat, coat, lunch, water, guidebook?"

Either Find A Way, Or Make One
Hannibal

CLIMBING SAFETY

Getting Started
Approaches
Climbers inappropriately dismiss approaches as trivial. In fact, accidents and deaths occur on the approach because climbers ignore the need for roping-up on difficult ground, carry things in their hands, wear ill-suited shoes that distract them, follow dead-end trails down to precipices, and ignore the threat of vertigo—the sudden loss of balance. Be alert while on approach.

> *Wizard Tip*—Never hold things in your hand(s) while on approach or descent unless the thing is essential to the task at hand—the rope or piece of protection needed to surmount or descend. People who lose their balance cling to the unimportant thing and fail to hold on for their lives.

If you have a helmet, wear it on difficult approaches and descents or if there is a falling rock hazard.

Assessing First Anchor
You seldom see climbers set anchors at the base of a climb—but they should. Climbers generally assume that the weight of the belayer is sufficient to prevent a falling leader from falling more than necessary. If the belayer is extra chunky, or the climber unusually light, this may be a safe assumption. More often than not, it is a poor bet to start off a lead climb without an anchor at the base.

Photo 8. Another trail to nowhere — Tunnel 2 at Clear Creek, Colo. Pack marks a dead-end, below which the trail drops off steeply.

A base anchor protects the leader against a more serious than anticipated fall and protects the belayer from being slammed against and dragged-up the rock. Slings around trees or substantial rocks are the most traditional base belays, but any nut-sling-bolt configuration can serve as a base anchor. The ideal base anchor is set below the waist of the belayer and is attached to the back of the belayer's harness. In the event of a significant leader fall, a front tie-in may cause the belayer to swing around, and perhaps let go of his belay.

Never Too Old—I had lead Eldorado Canyon's famous "Super Slab" route many times. As often as not, I fell on the first, steep corner pitch.

In the 1970s the climb sported many fixed pins, which guaranteed a virtual top rope for those not challenged by the clip-ins. Sometime later, the pins disappeared, leaving a much stouter lead—one that required holding on tight and carefully placing small stoppers.

In 1998, I decided to bring my new climbing friend "M" up this fine route. I weigh about 200 lbs, "M" much less. I warned him at the start that I could fall in the slippery dihedral, but I neglected to set an up-ward pull anchor to hold him down.

After jimmying a few small nuts, I told "M" that I would "go for it." Ignoring my fear, I spread eagled and slowly pushed off some dime-thin footholds while lie-backing and pulling on small edges. Just before reaching the final savior ledge, I peeled. I am sure "M" tried to stop my fall, but I found myself falling about 20 ft. SMACK went my right heel against the bottom ledge. "M" never had a chance to render a secure belay—my weight pulled him up and slammed him against the wall.

I gutted through the rest of the day, leading the whole of the route and some others on a gimped foot.

About eight months later, I lost the feeling in my lower right leg. I did not immediately link the fall to the lost feeling, but a visit to a neurologist and conversations with other climbers made it clear that my right leg neuropathy resulted from compressing my nerve in a fall. I had rushed into something that I could have made safe, and temporarily lost the sensation in my lower leg because of it.

Belaying the Leader

Climbers have a tacit fantasy that the leader's belayer is some sort of belay slave — 110% at attention and at service. The reality is that no one can concentrate on one thing for more than a few minutes; so the longer the lead-time, the greater the chance that the belayer will be distracted.

Photo 9. Another busy day of sport climbing.

To some, this is a terrifying revelation. You mean he is not really thinking about my well-being while I toil away on this 5.8b roof? No *dopissimus*, he is not.

How does the *Safety Buffalo* overcome this natural inattention? By talking to each other!

Verbal climbing signals are designed to be brief and distinct. By agreeing on the same language, partners have a better chance of avoiding the confusion encountered when the leader is toward the end of his rope, in a dangerous situation, or silenced by bad weather. These are common signals:

- "On Belay" or "Belay Is On" - belayer tells climber he is prepared to belay
- "Climbing" - climber begins to climb
- "Climb Away" - belayer reassures climber that he is belaying climber
- "Up Rope," "Tension," or "Take" - climber asks belayer to take up rope, take tension, take in slack, or hold me
- "Slack" - climber asks belayer to let out rope
- "Rope" - unfortunate though it may be, "Rope" can mean either take-up rope or let rope out; the belayer needs to be alert to the situation to know which context the climber means
- "Watch Me" - climber asks belayer to pay extra attention—he's going into a precarious situation and may fall
- "Clipped" - climber tells the belayer that he is safely clipped into a piece
- "Off Belay" or "Off" - climber is anchored and doesn't need a belay anymore
- "Thank You" - is like "10-4," OK, or I acknowledge you
- "Hauling" - used by a leader who is ready to haul a pack
- "Haul Away" - used by the second climber to state he is releasing a pack to be hauled
- "Lower Me" - the person on the rope is ready to be lowered

- "Lowering" – the belayer is lowering the climber
- "On Rappel" – the person is out of the anchor and into his rappel device
- "Off Rappel" or "Off" – the person is out of his rappel device
- "Safe" or "All Safe" – the person considers himself safe – because he is tied in, sheltered from rock, or for other reasons

Climbers who avoid using these brief phrases and instead chitchat compromise their safety because they create ambiguity.

There are also silent rope signals. Somewhere, someone set the rules for rope-tug signals – one if by sea, two if by land, or something. Since I can barely remember by own birthday, this *systematique* fails me. If the whipping wind is likely to prevent my belayer from hearing my belay signals or the belayer is likely to be out of earshot, I simply tell him in advance that the important moments in the lead are marked by the repetition of two sets of two sharp tugs on the rope. The sharpness tells the belayer I have an important message. The repetition tells the belayer that the message is no accident. So, after I secure myself to the new belay I tug twice, rest briefly, and then tug a second time. The belayer then takes me off belay, and I take up the slack until it is taut on his waist. When I can pull no more, I assume the dead weight is him, and I put him on belay. To let him know his belay is secure, I pull sharply twice, rest a moment, and then pull twice again.

Wizard Tip—Handy signals for noisy sport climb areas are the wave, thumbs-up and thumbs-down. To the *cognoscenti*, the wave means, "I'm off belay and OK," thumbs-up means "I'm OK," when signaled from leader to belayer, or "I'm ready to come up," when signaled from second to leader. Thumbs-down can mean something is wrong—or lower me down. Make sure you come to an agreement with your partner(s) before using any signals.

Any rational, memorable, rope-tug system can work—so long as both parties agree in advance to the signal, and the signal(s) are used consistently.

This simple system is functional for beginning and intermediate climbers because it is rare for them to be in impaired hearing situations.

Asleep at the Helm—"R" is a passionate climber. To assuage his passion, he will climb with anyone. When I met him, he was finally well enough mended to start climbing again. We climbed the "Turnkorner" on Colorado's Lumpy Ridge. During the climb, he told me about his injury.

He had hooked up with "Mike," a blind date—someone previously unknown to him—for a run up "Candyland" on Arizona's Granite Mountain. At the top of the climb, he found a difficult section. He struggled and struggled, finally committing to move ahead. To his surprise, when he fell, nothing caught him. He smacked a ledge some 40 ft below the vexing crux, breaking his legs. When "Mike" got to "R" during the rescue, "Mike" told "R" that he had assumed "R" was off belay because he never said anything and he was in the same place for so long. The failure by "R" to communicate caused him serious injury and life-long physical impairment.

The mechanics of belaying are simple, but made more complicated by the many options of belay devices.

The governing rule of belaying is never take the belay hand off the rope. Some modern devices allow the belayer to take his hand off the device, but it is not necessary and doing so develops bad habits in novices.

Photo 10. Climber models what not to do before catching a fall—his belay hand should be down.

Wizard Tip— Always have the belayer tied into the rope. Adopting this custom will safeguard against letting the rope fatally run through the belay device when climbing extra-long leads or descending extra-long pitches.

There are three common explanations for straying belay hands:
1. Inattention to belaying
2. Fluster resulting from the climber pulling the rope too fast or other lead excitement
3. The belayer inadvertently taking his hand off of the rope as he slides his hand back while giving slack or taking-in rope

Many things cause inattention to belaying:
- Talking to others
- Eating or drinking
- Fiddling with the anchor
- Managing tangled ropes
- Putting on/taking off clothes
- Hauling bags
- Other climbers anchoring while the leader leads
- Adverse conditions — too hot, cold, thirsty, hungry, tired, mad, scared...

The best way to avoid these distractions is to remedy everything that can be fixed prior to sending the leader off on his or her solemn mission, and by putting the belay at the forefront of the belayer's mind.

As indicated above, the burden of belaying is not solely the belayer's. It is a foolish leader who does not look down to check the status of the belay. If the leader suspects inattention, a cheery "Watch Me" brings the belay back into focus.

The same kind of leader vigilance goes a long way toward avoiding "Clip-In Panic." This is the panic the leader feels when he desperately tries to pull up rope for a clip-in, but finds the belayer asleep with a tangled or jammed rope. Leaders can avoid this unhappy situation by simply saying "Rope" or "Slack" prior to pulling up a rope for slack. The courtesy call also serves to offset the chance of the belayer letting go with his belay hand.

> *Wizard Tip*—Stop climbing with people who don't take belaying seriously.

The third belay-hand error, taking the hand off the rope while paying it in or out, is best avoided by practice and vigilance of the leader. Most people are embarrassed to be caught with their hand down, and a few well-timed reminders to "Keep Your Hand On The Rope," serve to get the belayer in the proper mode.

Leading
Equipment Selection
Leading is like a chess game. In climbing you and the rock serve as opponents. In planning a lead, you need to consider the weather, the descent, your gear, and your ability.

It is difficult and, at times, dangerous, to change clothes while climbing; so the best way to make yourself warmer or cooler is to use some clothes that can be modified. In cold weather, you can start out warmer with longer pants and shirts, and a hat. The pant leg and shirtsleeves can be rolled up if you get hot, and the hat can be quickly removed and clipped onto your harness or rack.

On a temperate day, you can dress lightly and tie a windshirt around your waist; bring a warm hat to be used at belays.

For longer climbs, you may want to bring water and an energy bar in a fanny pack or in a windbreaker pocket. Twelve- or 16-oz., plastic water bottles are essential for warmer weather. Affixing these with a short chord and duct tape enables you to hang them off your waist or a gear sling.

Gear selection is complex. Most guidebooks give general advice about size and types of racks used in an area and on specific climbs. These hints often favor a light rack. To maximize your security, you can double up on some sized pieces. The type of climb dictates that type of extra gear you should bring—face climbs and finger cracks lend themselves to pieces in the 1" and smaller size; hand cracks to 2" to 3.5"; and so on. If you are unsure of the specific extra protection to bring, adding four to six $1/8$"- to $1/2$"-wide stoppers is always cheap insurance—they weigh very little but have the potential to be very useful.

Adding two or three extra shoulder-length slings to your arsenal is equally good insurance. Oftentimes, especially on moderate climbs, you may encounter unforeseen tie-offs, or anchors that are well served by extra tie-in slings.

> *Wizard Tips*—Learn to identify the "feel" of a proper figure-eight tie-in by touch. Develop a habit of visually checking and touching your tie-in knot throughout the climbing day to be sure your tie-in is proper. There may not be such a thing as "too many" checks of tie-ins. Habitually checking your tie-in will save your life—at some point, everyone who climbs a lot looks down to see his or her knot half-tied.

> Also, look at your partner's knot throughout the day. If you are unsure why, read the story below (page 78), "R's First Time at Traditional Climbing."

Gear Selection — Racking Up

Choosing a rack configuration bears importantly on climbing safety, because a poor choice leads to poor lead performance, and less control over the climb. And fumbling can set the stage for an accident.

Photo 11. Climber demonstrates "touch-testing" of tie-in. Note antiquated swami belt.

> *Wizard Tip*—Clean and dry your climbing shoes at the base of each pitch. Dirt, grit, sand, and moisture on soles diminish performance and pose a hazard by increasing slip potential.

From the early 1970s until about 1990 climbers uniformly used "bandolier-style" slings to rack their hardware. More demanding climbers called for twin bandoliers, one around each shoulder with gear hung on each side.

With the advent of sport climbing in the 1990s, climbers became comfortable with hanging all of their gear off of their harnesses. This technique works well on sport climbs and on climbs with five to twelve pieces of hardware, but it is ill suited to climbers demanding a normal rack of 20 or more hardware pieces.

If you are right handed, you will want to hang your primary bandolier over your right shoulder, so the gear dangles on your left side. There are many ways to rack hardware on a bandolier. My style is to rack the larger pieces toward the back of the bandolier, with each piece on its own carabiner. The gates face in, toward your body, and up. This allows the leader to grab a piece by pinching his thumb from the inside toward the outside.

> *Wizard Tip*—Leave your wedding band, watch, and any other jewelry at home or secure in a fanny pack. Climbs ruin both wedding bands and fingers with bands. If you wear earrings, consider the risk of getting a loop caught in something during a fall.

Routes that demand more than 18 pieces of hardware require more complex racking. In this case, you may want to bunch two or three smaller pieces on a single biner. Extra-large biners serve this purpose well. On very demanding climbs, you may find yourself putting five or ten wired stoppers on a biner. This technique is an efficient way to carry wired stoppers, but remember, with every piece you add, the price of losing the biner by dropping it goes up.

The most demanding traditional climbs call for using dual bandoliers, one on each shoulder. With this set-up, a leader can comfortably carry an arsenal of 40 or more pieces of hardware. The dual bandoliers also have the advantage of balancing your weight distribution; so the rack does not upset you.

Remember, each piece of gear will require some attaching sling and/or carabiners. As a rule of thumb, your rack will need two carabiners for each piece of hardware, and a total number of slings or quickdraws equal to about two-thirds the total pieces of hardware. Under this formula, a 24-piece rack needs 48 carabiners, and 16 slings or quickdraws.

Gear Placement

People write entire books about gear placement. Here is a summary:

- The integrity of the rock governs the integrity of a placement. A good placement in bad rock is a bad placement.
- The more metal on rock, the better the placement.
- A placement that can be pulled out is not a good placement. The direction of pull for the placement must serve the direction of a likely fall. Use appropriate extensions to assure a piece will not pull.
- As a secondary consideration, be mindful that gear needs to be snug, but not so snug that that

it cannot be removed. Too many stuck pieces sap a team's energy.

Wizard Tip—The Fail-Safe Placement Cluster. Whenever the leader climbs far enough above her last piece such that a fall will land her on the ground, she must re-establish herself in the lead chain. To do this, she must place enough gear in a cluster or string to prevent any catastrophic failure. When possible, place two or three pieces together, or in a short string, to guard against catastrophic failure. By definition, one piece cannot be failsafe—it defies the safety requirement for redundant systems.

Photo 12. Well-placed hex in crack.

Placement Planning

Gear planning does not end when the leader starts up a pitch. While leading long pitches, especially cracks, it becomes obvious that the climb requires more of one certain-sized piece than another. Before you start, and as you go, study the pitch to determine which gear needs to be conserved for higher up and which gear can safely be used lower down.

Photo 13. Well-placed tri-cam in boulders.

Fixed Gear

Every climber relies on fixed bolts, pitons, slings, and chains, but before doing so, you must judge their integrity.

Wizard Tip— A minimally sufficient anchor has two perfect or near perfect pieces and two or more substantial slings, chains, or combinations thereof. Avoid subminimal anchors at all costs by adding to them or by foreshortening or lengthening leads to benefit from better belay stations.

With few exceptions, fixed pitons and slings are not to be trusted. There are two basic types of pins, "chrome-moly," (chromium molybdenum) or hard pins, and "soft" iron. Chrome-moly has a dark black appearance and is indeed hard. "Soft" iron has a light-steel appearance. Chrome-moly pins are designed to be rigid and to be used over and over again. Soft pins are less expensive and are often left as fixed gear, especially in Europe. The only time a pin may be reliable is when it is pounded into a horizontal crack or directly down, snugly into a crack. One especially dangerous type of pin is the "old-soft-iron-angle" with the welded ring. These pins date back 30 or more years, and the quality of the rings is uncertain. If you run into a ring pin, the best option is to tie-off the shaft with a girth-hitch or slipknot rather than to clip the ring. Up until the late 1970s, some climbers carried small rock hammers to test pins, but pins are no longer very common, and this custom is no longer in use. If you climb in piton-infested areas, consider carrying a small hammer and learning ironmongery.

The main exception to the "don't trust the pin rule" is in the Shawangunks of New York State. The "Gunks" boast thousands of 'em that are relied on daily.

New fresh slings may be safe, but given the chance, always back up both fixed pins and slings.

All bolts consist of an insert into the rock and an attachment device—usually a hanger. There are two main types of bolt inserts:

- Mechanical bolts come in two principal varieties:
  - *Compression* bolts consist of a rod, dowel, nail, or piton that is pounded into a drilled hole; the compression of the insert provides most of the integrity of the bolt.
  - *Expansion* bolts involve a metal piece that expands as a wrench tightens a hex-nut.
- Glue-ins consist of the insert and glue.

The study of fixed bolts is complex. There are at least 11 different styles of rock inserts, and as many or more different hangers. The American Safe Climbing Association website (http://www.safeclimbing.org) supplies a detailed summary of bolting and insert styles. The following summary reviews the safety issues involving bolts:

- Inspect all fixed bolts before using.
- Never pound a bolt to test it.
- In general, all modern bolt inserts on sport climbs are reliable. This is not equally true of the hangers. A basic sport-climbing bolt inspection consists of assuring that the insert is $3/8"$ or $½"$ in diameter, checking the cap-nut or screw that affixes the hanger to the insert, and analyzing the hanger. The cap-nut or screw must be tight. Most people check these to finger-tightness. Hangers are the most problematic part of the typical sport bolts. First ascentionists can and do use homemade hangers and "cold shuts." Cold shuts are hangers de-

signed for construction and are bought in hardware stores. They may be left with open mouths, "shut–cold" with a hammer, or shut and welded. No matter the state, none are reliable and they should be replaced or backed-up at every opportunity.

❑ You can identify homemade hangers by the lack of a trademark and uneven quality. Generally these are cut from angle iron. The lack of quality control poses a failure hazard and the angled edges pose a cut hazard. They may cut you open if you fall past them.

❑ Bolt hangers on sport-climbing anchors are particularly problematic. Cold shuts are the worst. They wear quickly, leaving dangerous wear grooves that weaken the already substandard hanger. These should be replaced, or at the very least, climbers should add repair links and/or descent rings to the cold shut to diminish the chance of catastrophic failure.

❑ Bolts on traditional climbs can date back as far as the 1940s and they pose great danger. All ¼"-diameter inserts are unsafe. Granite areas frequently have ¼"-"Rawl Drive," buttonhead bolts which pull easily. The other type of common substandard bolt is the "Star Dryvin," nail-in bolt. These come in ¼"- and $3/8$"-diameter shafts, and are often seen in the Colorado-Utah desert areas. Star Dryvins are secured by a nail in the sleeve. Like the Rawl, these are not suitable for rock climbing and should never be trusted with your life.

❑ Unique to sandstone, climbers drill $3/8$"-plus-sized holes and pound-in "drilled pins." The drilled pins are $3/8$" US Army soft-angle pitons that have cut off tips or $3/8$" chrome-moly pitons called baby angles. Many people have fallen on this type of protection and survived, but it is difficult to be sure of the quality of these pieces. A safety inspection involves checking the angle of the hole relative to the rock-face angle, trying to wiggle it with your fingers, looking for cracks or deformation, and checking to see if the placement has an epoxy seal.

Some climbers assert that the hole should face slightly downward to keep water out, but this is patently unnerving. If the pin is driven perpendicular to the rock face, or at a slight, upward angle, if there is no deformation or cracking of the head and an epoxy seal, these bolts may be reliable, but they can never be relied on to the degree that modern expansion bolts can be relied upon.

❑ One final note on drilled pins—tie off the shaft if they are the old ring-pins made for the US Army. If the girth hitch tie-off looks insecure, instead tie a slipknot around the shaft and run a loop of the free end through the ring. Clip a loop from the slipknot and the loop that runs through the ring into a biner for your clip-in.

❑ The placement of glue-ins requires refined knowledge and should not be attempted without detailed study and preparation.

□ Attachments to bolt hangers, slings, chains, and rings, can all be dangerously worn and should always be inspected prior to use.

Photo 14. Soft iron on the left, chrome-moly on the right. Note welded-descending ring of indeterminate quality on left.

Wizard Tip—Carry a 3/8" wrench in your pack for sport climbs. You may want to tighten down a cap-nut for your own safety and as a community service—but don't overtighten.

Wizard Tip—Climbers erroneously assume that because fixed gear has been used before, for years, it "must be safe." Bad mistake. The Yosemite climb, "Anchors Away," was not misnamed. Learn to identify the "minimally sufficient anchor"—an anchor with at least two bombproof pieces that is equalized with two connectors in good condition. The connectors can be chains, biners, or slings.

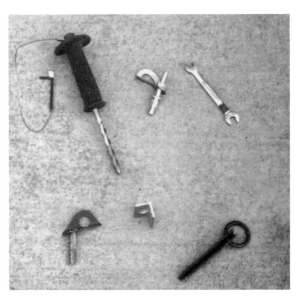

Photo 15. Modern hand drill with modern expansion bolt upper row. Lower row (L to R) has unsafe nail-drive bolt, dangerous homemade hanger, and sawed army angle.

Photo 16. Clockwise from upper left: <u>dangerous</u> cold shut, OK repair link, painted "leaver biner," <u>safe</u> cast-descent ring, and questionable welded ring.

Photo 17. Industrial cold-shuts on a typical sport anchor. These hangers are not designed for climbing and should always be used with caution.

Backing-up Gear

Climbers enforce an unwritten rule forbidding gear placement on sport routes. You can use stick clips, hang, and rehearse, but if a stopper minimizes a fall, that's a serious code violation. Go figure. People who put up sport routes make mistakes. They may place a bolt that's reachable and useful only for those over 6'2", or they may skip a bolt because they need beer money that day. None of that should preclude a climber from placing his own gear on sport routes. To be *Ultrasafe*, always carry a minimum of five or six nuts or cams on sport routes. These should span the $1/16"$ to $1"$ range.

Photo 18. Modern bolt hangers attached to appropriate expansion bolts. The stress configuration would be better if one bolt were placed about 6" to 8" below the other, but this ideal is seldom seen.

Whenever possible, especially with questionable fixed gear, always back-up the piton, bolt or sling. At the very least, the back-up piece may be helpful to prevent an accidental clip-out when the falling leader passes by.

There are four common Clip Devices used to connect protection to the rope: (1) single carabiners, (2) slings with carabiners, (3) quickdraws, and (4) slings girth-hitched through protection.

Multi-Clips are ways of duplicating attachments to protection to guard against accidental un-clipping. Climbers take unexpectedly long falls when their rope falls across a biner's gate or torques biners causing the biner to break. To guard against these accidents, critical clip-ins, such as those at cruxes, should include one or more of the following safe-guards:

- Use locking biners at one or both ends of a clip to a bolt.
- Use double biners, gates flipped and reversed.
- If a bolt is extra large, it may accommodate two quickdraws, biners flipped and reversed in the bolt hanger. A fall may damage or break one or more of these biners; so each situation must be evaluated.
- If a bolt hanger is smooth-edged, and no other means of back-up is available, you may girth-hitch a 5/8" sling into the bolt along with a quickdraw. These slings may fail if the edge of the bolt is sharp.

Protecting the Second is critical on overhangs and traverses. If a climb poses a swinging fall for the second climber, always safeguard the second against an impacting fall or rope-cut. To do this, the leader may have to place extra gear and advise the second how he can reduce the fall hazard.

> *Wizard Tip*—Some leaders take delight in the fear seconds experience on traverses. These folks may give a little extra slack to the second to make him feel the thrill of the lead. Beware this malevolence and insist on the best possible belay.

Learning to rest without hanging on gear is important to being safe because not all climbs have gear that allow rests where needed. The ideal rest allows both arms to hang down, but these are uncommon. Climbers need to find a position where they can lock-off the various limbs while alternately resting one limb. At times, climbers rest their head on the rock as a pivot point and let their arms hang free.

Photo 19. Locking biners on sport bolt.

Story — *R's First Time at Traditional Climbing.* R was a talented sport climber with little traditional experience. We set off to climb the classic "Tulgey Wood" route on Devil's Tower. To add some spice, R took off onto the 5.11 variation, "A Bridge Too Far." He climbed it quickly and flawlessly. A few pitches higher, we stood close to each other, and I looked at his waist in disbelief. He had never completed the finish to his figure-eight tie-in. Had he fallen anywhere below, or leaned back too readily on the anchor, he would have dropped to his death.

Photo 20. Two quickdraws on a bolt—less than ideal.

Downclimbing while on belay is just as important as resting and for the same reason—often there is no safe piece for lowering. When on unprotected ground, always establish your ability to reverse moves if the climbing proves untenable.

Once you learn to take rests in the natural spots, place gear where it is available, not to linger on unprotected spots, and to power through cruxes, you will be on your way to "floating" up climbs at your level of competence.

Photo 21. In a pinch, climbers can back-up a sport clip with a girth-hitch through the bolt. Sling could break.

Hanging is poor style, but if hanging on a secure piece saves you from a dangerous fall, by all means hang. Remember though, if you always resort to hanging as the solution to overly challenging climbs, you will be ill-prepared to face dangerous climbs that lack convenient hangs.

Falling is an art. Watch someone fall on his or her first day of climbing and you will see how artless it can be. To "fall well" the climber plans the moment and trajectory of the fall. Best to avoid hitting the head and spine. If you must take a long winger, try to land on your feet if you are going to hit the ground or a ledge. Remember, falls off traverses, lay-backs, and underclings are the most dangerous because they are more likely to result in upper-body impacts (Dill, 2001). The best falls are planned with the belayer; the most dangerous are spontaneous. To be *Ultrasafe*, you should climb with enough control to anticipate potential falls. Tell the belayer to "Watch Me." Climbers are known to grab the lead rope while they fall in some ill-conceived effort to self-arrest. Never try to "pinch" a loop of rope to foreshorten a fall — this effort generally results in a burnt rope and burnt hands. In a similar vein, be extra careful when you clench the rope in your mouth prior to clipping a piece of protection — if you fall in this posture, you may pull out a bunch of teeth.

> *Wizard Tip* — Short falls are not necessarily safe falls. Beware of any fall that will result in your body contacting the rock. Because easier climbs are often less steep than hard climbs, falls off easier climbs can result in more injuries in comparison to falls off steep and overhanging hard climbs.

Climbing near the ground, easy ground, and ropes tangled in feet all pose fall hazards unrecognized by novices and under-appreciated by experienced climbers. Many climbers assume that because they are near the ground, they can run-out the start of a lead. This is wrong — the proximity of the ground poses a higher hazard than the hazard posed by a "clean" fall higher up. Remember, it's still a ground fall.

Easy ground on climbs lulls climbers into thinking they need not place protection. Climbers must always place gear at sufficiently close intervals to prevent injurious falls. Just because climbing is easy does not mean you will not slip on loose rock or suffer from a lapse of attention.

Ropes tangled in the climber's feet or legs pose a third under-appreciated hazard. The rope should run in front of the leader to prevent the climber from inverting during a fall. Make sure it never runs through your legs or ends up twisted around one leg.

Loose Rock poses a hazard as you stand on it, grip it, place protection in it, and if it is overhead. The ancient "three-point" rule is designed to protect you from falling due to loose rock underfoot and in-hand. The three-point rule says never move up unless three limbs are on the rock. Visually inspecting and tapping hand and foot holds also gives you notice of loose rock hazards.

Before you place gear, you must study the rock:
- ❑ Are you on a detached pillar, flake, or ledge that may collapse or break when you touch it or place gear in it?
- ❑ Does the crack before you have loose flakes in it that will collapse upon loading?
- ❑ Are the walls of the crack sandy or otherwise fractured such that a piece of gear will pull out upon loading?

The best way to avoid rock falling from above is to be aware of area conditions and seasonal rock fall. Spring is generally the height of the rock-fall season due to the "freeze-thaw" cycle. Connecting with locals is critical—they will tell you that Middle Cathedral and Glacier Point Apron in Yosemite Valley are bowling alleys, that ice streams off The Bulge Wall in Eldorado Canyon, and that the base of the Space Boyz Wall in Potrero Chico is a death zone.

> *Wizard Tip*—Experienced sandstone climbers are the masters of loose rock. They compress loose holds and pull straight down on holds rather than out on them. These techniques serve on all types of bad rock.
>
> A second tip for soft-rockers: sandstone is substantially weakened by moisture. Allow two or more days of drying before stepping onto rain or snow-drenched sandstone.

Setting the Lead Anchor entails the following steps:

- Secure yourself by clipping into fixed gear or by placing two substantial pieces and clipping into them. You need to use two separate slings, a cordellette, or the rope to clip in. A single sling into an anchor is never failsafe. Once you are into two quality pieces, refine nut anchors by adding one or two additional pieces before calling off-belay and bringing your partner up.
- Always tie the rope into the anchor. This is the safest practice—it firmly attaches the climbing team together and to the anchors.
- Call yourself off belay.
- If the anchor includes less than perfect pieces or there are concerns about the direction of pull, equalize the anchor using multiple slings, a chordellette, or a bowline on a bight knot.
- Re-attach yourself to the perfected anchor and bring up the slack in the rope.
- Belay up the second.

> *Wizard Tip*—Avoid futzing with the anchor while belaying. The anchor needs to be well set prior to the climber's launch.

Photo 22. Minimally sufficient anchor—three good pieces equalized with a three-bighted bowline.

Following
Belaying the Second

Safety and etiquette call for a belay with little slack and no tension. Some leaders like to motivate their second by leaving substantial loops of rope at the second's waist. This is both un-fun and unsafe. When a second is on a traverse, treat this like a lead, with careful play of slack and tension to prevent unnecessarily long falls.

If the leader thinks the second is likely to fall, he or she may run the belay rope through an anchor piece to provide a pulley effect. Ideally, this piece will be bombproof and above the belayer's head for maximum leverage.

Photo 23. Chordellette tied with 8.8-mm rope—useful for multi-piece anchors, especially for top-ropes.

> *Wizard Tip*—Novices invariably try to hook a finger through bolt hangers when they are scared. This is a good way to lose the sensation in a finger or the finger itself. Resist the temptation to do this.

Rope Management

To prevent rope jams, the leader should stack the rope at his or her feet while taking it in, or stuff 8′ to 12′ loops (lap coils) through a hanging sling to prevent rope jams that may distract him or her. If there is a rope jam, tie off the climber before messing with the jam.

85

Photo 24. Climber is double-roped to prevent pendulum fall. If a fall would be serious, climber could leave protection on right. In this case, he would untie from the right rope when he arrives at a safe stance with protection, pull the rope through the right piece, and re-tie. Tie is antiquated swami belt.

When the Second Leaves the Anchor he should wait to take out the last pieces until he is certain he is on belay. If there are substantial fixed pieces, to expedite the climb he may stayed clipped into the fixed pieces and unclip the back-up, removable protection while he waits for the taut-line belay.

> *Wizard Tip—*To aid rapid, sport climb clip-ins, many people girth-hitch a shoulder-length sling through the front of their harness. (If you use a back-up swami belt,

this must be hitched too.) Be sure the hitch includes the lower leg-loop portion too. While this technique is well suited to sport climbing, it is not well suited to multi-pitch traditional routes. For these, always tie in with the rope to one or more pieces of the anchor.

Hauling a daypack — as opposed to wearing it — enhances the enjoyment of the second and may conserve the team's strength, but hang-ups can create safety problems. The most common hang-up occurs after the leader establishes the lead belay and hauls the bag. If the bag becomes stuck, tie it off. When the second reaches the bag to release it, be sure the second is tied-off to the belay onto two or more safe pieces of protection before hauling the bag. Beware of hauling and belaying at the same time.

Gear Removal

Be wary of nuts and cams flying into your face upon fall or removal. They can break a tooth or injure an eye. Removing out-of-sight gear can be especially dangerous; the trajectory when you pull it out may cause it to hit you in the face.

If gear is very difficult to get out, consider leaving it. This is an especially good tactic if you have a long way to go. Sapped strength early on may compromise your safety later when you need the reserves. Climbers who only carry cams are unlikely to give those expensive birds up; so this is another argument for carrying some cheaper gear — hexes, for example.

Transitions

Transitions from climbing to anchor pose a number of hazards:

- The partners can be confused in the tangle of ropes and slings and inadvertently un-clip one another.

- One climber may unwittingly remove a piece of the anchor as he fiddles with the anchor system.

- Novice climbers have mistakenly untied on their first multi-pitch climb because sport climbing conditioned them to think that after a pitch is over, they untie.

- Climbers may drop the rack or rope as they pass gear. This may cause the team to be stranded and precipitate the need for a rescue.

- If one member of the team is too slow, the other partner may become cold or otherwise lose his or her momentum. This could heighten the risk of a bad decision or leader fall.

- Other climbing teams may ask to use the same anchor that you are using. Their added weight or a fall may exceed the strength of the anchor, or one of the many climbers hanging on the anchor may inadvertently un-clip someone from the anchor. Beware of sharing anchors.

Wizard Tip—If you are untied on a big ledge, or you are at the edge of a cliff, sit, never stand. Vertigo, the body's sudden loss of balance, can precipitate a catastrophic fall for the un-anchored.

The second should never take his anchoring for granted and should closely study the anchor and his attachment to it.

> *Wizard Tip*—When an aboveground pitch starts off with hard moves, clip the leader through the highest, solid piece of the anchor. If this clip creates rope drag, un-clip it once the climber places bombproof pieces higher up.

Descents

Skiers know that the last runs of the day are the most dangerous—fatigue taxes mind and body. Few climbers arm themselves with the same *caveat*, but we should. Descents are hazardous because of the fall exposures and because we are tired, and often self-satisfied with the day's conquests.

Sport Climb Descents

Sport climb descents are dangerous and the setting of some accidents. Sport climbs may be exited by walk-off, rappel, or lowering. The current custom to lower off has been the cause of a number of deaths. When a climber lowers off a fixed anchor, he clips into the anchor, unties, threads the lead rope, ties back in, and then instructs the belayer to lower him. Deaths have occurred when the climber mistakenly thinks he is attached to the anchor and when the belayer somehow fails to lower the climber. The root cause of many of these accidents is failed communication between climber and belayer.

The way to reduce these accidents is to take the belayer out of the equation whenever possible. The climber should attach herself to the anchor, thread the rope herself, and rappel herself off the route. By setting out with the assumption that she controls everything, there is little room for tragic fatal mistakes.

> *Wizard Tips*—Rappelling and cleaning sport climbs poses risks different from those incurred when lowered. A tired climber may loose his grip. One way to recover gear is to pull both ropes up through all of the gear, and leave it for the second to clean while he climbs. If a climb is especially hard, the second may unclip on the way up and clean on his way down.

A second unfortunate accident type arises from ropes that are too short. Increasingly, sport climbs are set to 100 ft. These require 60-m ropes for safe, single-line, lowering or rappelling. In the 1990s a number of climbers were seriously hurt when their belayers let the rope-end run through the belay device causing the climber to fall 20 ft or more.

This accident type reinforces the need to always tie the belayer in or to knot the loose end of the rope.

Sport-climb descents are critically dangerous and require a high degree of attention. The social atmosphere of sport climbing encourages distraction and contributes to the likelihood of an accident.

Rappelling off Traditional Climbs

Rappelling off traditional climbs entails unique and common hazards:

- Climbers fall off ledges while in transition to rappels.
- Climbers pull themselves up, hand-over-hand, to retrieve stuck ropes or gear, and their grip slips.

❑ Climbers fail to secure themselves to their rappel device. When they unclip from the anchor, they sail to the earth.

❑ Climbers misjudge the integrity of anchors, and the anchor pulls out once it is weighted.

❑ Every novice climber manages to get a shirt or sweater suck into the rappel device, causing embarrassment, an accident or both.

❑ A tired rappeller can lose his grip and fall.

❑ A single rope, or more likely, double ropes attached by a knot, becomes stuck while being pulled down, stranding the climbers, or inspiring some desperate self-rescue. In the self-rescue, one brave climber climbs up the stuck rope hoping to find the stuck knot before it cuts loose and sends him or her sailing.

❑ Climbers incorrectly tie the knot joining the two rappel ropes, causing catastrophic failure.

❑ Team fails to tie knots in the end of the rope(s), and one member flies off the unsecured end.

❑ Rocks dislodge, fall, and cut ropes during rappels or while climbers are pulling the ropes down.

❑ Hot days make for hot rappels. Extra-hot ropes and rappel devices can cause climbers to let go of their rappel. This is as much a threat on sport climbs as on traditional climbs.

❑ Climbers may inadvertently let go of a rappel while trying to untangle a knot in the rappel ropes.

Wizard Tip—When on a hanging belay, use a "stirrup-sling" to step up toward the anchor so that you unweight the sling that attaches you to the anchor. This is

> done after your rappel is set up. The stirrup allows you to hold onto the rappel with one hand, and then use the second hand to unclip your tie—a tense moment. This technique is especially useful on hanging sport-climb anchors.

The protocol for safely checking a rappel is as follows:

1. Analyze the anchor. It must have at least two excellent pieces and two fresh slings, rappel rings, or chains. If it does not, enhance it. Beware of welded descent rings—these may be sub-standard. The welds are not certified and should never be trusted. Cast rings have a continuous piece of metal. In contrast, welded rings have a raised bead or ridge. In either case, never thread a rope through one piece of anything.

2. At times, climbers face the prospect of rappelling off of slings rather than through the preferred double-descent rings. When forced to do this, make sure you avoid sudden movements of rope through sling—this can cause rope burn, or in extreme cases, it can cause catastrophic failure when the slings burn through.

3. Thread the rope through the anchor slings or rings. If the single line has no marked middle, match the ends in your hand and pull the rope through to find the middle.

4. If it is a double-rope rappel, tie the two ends together using a double-fisherman's bend or a figure-eight follow-through. Use an overhand knot or second double-fisherman's bend to tie off the tails of the main knot.

5. Tie knots in the lower end of the rope to prevent anyone from rappelling off the ends.
6. Lap coil the rope and throw it off of the ledge. Yell "rope" a few times to alert those below before you throw.
7. While still clipped in, attach your rappel device to the ropes. If the belay ledge has numerous cracks, trees, or rocks, which may catch the double-rope knot when pulled, consider having the last rappeller lower the knot to below the ledge lip. If you do this, you add an extra fall hazard because the last person will have to climb down to below the knot level to start his or her rappel. Most people overcome this hazard by connecting their rappel device below the knot while they are still at the anchor and hand-over-handing down to below the knot. This is dangerous. To be *Ultrasafe*, you must thread a long sling through the anchor. Once you have climbed down and weighted the anchor below the knot, pull the lanyard through the anchor to recover it. This *Ultrasafe* technique is only used when climbers are extremely tired or scared.
8. With the rappel ropes in hand, unclip yourself from the anchor. Conduct one final survey of your anchor, the rope knot, and your connection to the rappel device prior to undoing your last piece.
9. When you arrive at the anchor below, don't detach from the rappel until you are safely into at least two substantial pieces of protection, using two separate slings. Note: getting into

an anchor on overhanging or steep rock can be unnerving. Best to pace yourself and check everything twice before unclipping from the rappel.

Wizard Tip—Consider clipping your rappel device into a second biner or quickdraw attached to your harness. This may safeguard against the rare time when your primary clip-in fails. You may also double clip belay devices if a leader wants reassurance.

First Day in the Desert—"H" was a wiry sport dude, able to run up 5.11b clip-ups. I had always wanted to climb the Priest in Castle Valley, Utah, and we agreed to conquer it together. He felt uncomfortable on the traditional stuff; so I lead the whole climb. After patting ourselves on the back on the summit, we headed down the rappels I was first down from the top. When "H" arrived, he quickly unclipped from his figure-eight and stood like a proud father on the small ledge. I was aghast to see he had never clipped into the anchor. "H" was accustomed to *terra firma* at the bottom of single-pitch sport routes; so he never considered that each anchor station on a multi-rappel descent requires the climber to anchor before unclipping from the rappel.

Caution—Many novice rappellers use back-up knots like prussiks or heddens. These knots slide down the rope, and ideally, if the rappeller lets go of the rope—and the knot—the knots catch the fall. As often as not, the scared rappeller clings to the knot, undermining its utility. If the knot does its job, rappellers often let these knots get away, causing a hang-up. If none of those bad things happen, a shirttail catches in the knot. If you are insecure about rappelling, have a friend belay you down rappels until you feel comfortable without the back-up. You will see that experienced climbers never use a back-up. If tired, they simply use rappel devices with higher degrees of resistance—a tube or sticht plate. For more on the problems with rappel safeties, see Gary Storrick's website, "My Internet Post on Rappel Safeties."

Traditional Climb Walk-Offs

If you told the average climber that you were going soloing, un-roped, he would beg off. But climbers routinely climb unroped on descents and approaches, and these exposed positions are common accident settings (American Alpine Club, 2001). Dill (2001) reports that many Yosemite Valley accidents involve climbers in various un-roped conditions:

- Loose rock, sand, wetness, and darkness all contribute to climbers slipping on easy ground.
- Climbers choose not to take off their packs to either haul or boost them over hard sections when faced with a difficult step. The added weight causes a fall.
- Climbers may reach down for a shoelace, a dropped water bottle, or another item, and tumble.
- In a moment of lost thought, climbers may ignore the nature of vertigo—the momentary loss of balance—and fall on "easy ground" or off a secure ledge.
- Previous teams may beat paths down dead-ends, misleading inexperienced climbers into dangerous outposts.
- A stinging plant or animal may startle the tyro, causing a tumble.

Retreat and Accidents

Retreat and Self-Rescues

If you put safety first, there is no shame in retreat. Retreats and self-rescue generally involve lowering to a rappel station and coming down. The critical safety issue here is finding or making a place to safely lower yourself from. The problem is three-fold: climbers are often faced with lowering off of a single piece; climbers are cheap and do not want to leave gear; and the safest rigging is often complex. Consider the following methodologies:

- On climbs that are easy for you, down-climb and remove gear as you go.
- On climbs with reliable fixed bolts or other gear, simply leave a single or double biner and carefully have your partner lower you down.
- On climbs with substandard gear, you may consider "aid" climbing up to a known piece of protection, fixed anchor, or site with probable good protection placements. Aiding-up requires making girth-hitch-joined shoulder-length slings for use as aiders.
- If it is not possible to get up to a good piece or anchor, you may use your substandard piece to lower down to a better piece, rearrange the rope, and lower off the acceptable piece. If the substandard piece is so questionable that you do not want to lower off it at all, judge whether or not you can down-climb from it using the upper piece as a last chance back-up. This is a poor gamble.
- All of these techniques call for an attentive belayer.

In rare cases, a climber may dangle away from the rock, requiring him to ascend the rope. In this case, fashion ascenders out of slings. Tie yourself some hedden knots, attach waist and legs, and up you go to a place where you can establish a retreat.

Accidents are addressed in the Preparation Chapter. For a full treatment, seek other information sources.

Good Judgment Comes from Bad Experience.
John Dill, Yosemite National Park Chief Rescue Ranger

PEOPLE

You

No single factor has more bearing on climber safety than a climber's own attitude, quirks and conduct. Some manage to hurt themselves on simple top-ropes, while others spend entire careers soloing difficult routes without a single injury — the individual makes all the difference.

Climbing can be a few isolated days of top-roping during a year, or it can be a way of life. Those who explore and advance in climbing find it to be as intellectually and spiritually challenging as it is physically challenging. To grow and be safe in climbing, you will face all of the most sensitive aspects of personality and personal development.

Personality, distractions, and thought process all bear importantly on climbing safety:

Personality
❖ Leadership
Climbers face hard decisions. Sometimes a team makes the hard decisions, but more often, one partner assumes the leadership role.

Usually the more experienced partner makes the most difficult decisions. This is especially true when the decision involves leading a pitch and the decision-maker intends to take the risk.

> *Wizard Tip* — Leader is not the same as dictator. A capable leader is open to relevant information and is accountable for his or her decisions. The climbing community recognizes leaders as people who consistently make good decisions, are brave, and who climb well.

Consider if you are well served by acknowledging which partner is the leader.

❖ Denial
Denial serves us well. Denying traumatic events allows people to see beyond them, and often to surpass them. Denying stated limitations allows many to achieve remarkable successes. The climber who puts safety first, however, cannot deny his own limitations or limitations imposed by outside factors such as adverse weather or rock conditions. Be wary of your partner's or your own denial.

❖ Fear
To a greater or lesser extent, climbers are attracted to fear. Some seek a climactic fearsome event and then leave climbing. Dedicated climbers get to know, control, and abide fear. It is OK to give in to fear when a safe retreat is available. If you climb for a while, you inevitably will find yourself in a dangerous and fearsome situation from which you cannot safely retreat. Your arms may turn to mush, your belly may tighten up, your legs may "sewing machine," and worse. To avoid injury or death, you must control your fear. Here are some strategies to control fear:
  ❑ Try to place a good piece of protection. If none are available, take second or third best.

❑ Find a rest position from which you can study the coming moves.

❑ Visualize the moves.

❑ Tentatively try the moves, reversing them back to your rest.

❑ Keep talking to the belayer. Tell him to take in slack when it appears and to pay it out when necessary. One extra foot of slack, or inadvertent tension, may contribute to an avoidable bad fall.

❑ After study and trial, and before you have sapped your strength, go for it.

❑ Only attempt the move when you see a sequence that either takes you to a piece of protection or to a stable rest from which you can launch another advance.

❑ If it helps, silently or overtly talk to yourself. You may even benefit from describing the moves out loud yourself—or saying "think-think" and "you'll be OK."

❑ When you get to a safe spot, tell your partner that you are OK—"all safe." He or she can then momentarily ease attention and save it for later.

> *Wizard Tip*—Study all retreat options. Be inventive. Remember, climbing is not war. You are better off retreating than incurring injury or death.

❖ Anxiety

People who work around aircraft, particularly helicopters, know that the loud whir of engines causes many to move faster. Wind, bad weather, and anxiety also cause some climbers to speed up, a disposition that can contribute to accidents.

❖ Passivity
A 1970s climbing luminary often told me, "The mountains don't care." You must take an active role in your own safety and that of others if you want to avoid accidents and injuries. Pretending everything will "turn out OK" may be beneficial after the onset of a mishap, but not before. At the same time, beware of undermining the confidence of your team—climbing takes courage and you can never eliminate all of the risk.

❖ Recklessness
Do you run in front of cars? Speed? Violate the law? Congratulations, you are reckless! If you ignore safety and embrace danger, climbing will likely kill or maim you.

❖ Ambition
Climbers must measure ambition against peril. If you are overly ambitious, safety is unlikely to come first.

❖ Casual
"Off the couch." That describes flawless ascents made with little preparation or thought. It is inspiring to climb "off the couch" every once in a while, but lack of preparation is unsafe and will increase your hazard exposure.

The mind's tendency to assume the present conditions will continue unchanged also leads to inattentiveness. Overcome the tendency to think the weather or rock conditions at the start of a climb will continue throughout the climb.

> *Too casual?—A Story.* B had finished an outstanding season in Eldorado Canyon. Before he went home for the summer he wanted to climb the classic Anthill Direct. B was a solid 5.10 climber, but he broke his ankle when he fell at the top of the first pitch, a 5.8 crack. He explained that he just stopped paying attention. Later that summer, B's friend S was finishing his first Yosemite season with a cruise up Sentinel — the Steck Salathe. S fell on the first 5.7 slab pitch. He had placed little gear because it was "so easy." S landed on his face, virtually wiping it off.

❖ Cheapness

At times climbers are forced to leave entire racks worth thousands of dollars to beat a safe descent or retreat. If you ever hesitate to leave gear because of the cost, ask yourself the dollar value of your life. If the answer is that your life is worth more than the gear you hesitate to leave, then leave the gear.

> *Story—Death in the Alps.* Friend "O" and partner set off to conquer the American Direct on the Dru. Upon seeing an Italian team sail some 3,000 ft to their deaths, the partners decided to retreat. "O," the heavier of the two said he would back-up a single-pin retreat with a nut. If "M," the partner made it down OK, "O" would recover his back-up nut and rappel down. "M" made it down OK, but the single pin pulled on "O," sending him to his death.

❖ Committed

The further climbers travel and the more they spend, the more they feel obligated to "go for it." Don't let your embedded time and costs in a trip overrule your good judgment.

103

Distractions
❖ Relieving Yourself

Relieving yourself on a climb can be hazardous to your health. In modesty, you can walk onto an unstable rock shelf, into an avalanche zone, or into a rock-fall zone. Also, unbuckling your harness exposes you to falls during the time you are unbuckled and in the event you forget to completely re-buckle. Similarly, untying exposes you to being untied during your "private moment" and to forgotten or faulty tie-ins. So, be careful when you have to go.

Thought Process
❖ Deliberate Thought

Consciously or subconsciously, expert climbers think deliberately. They plan climbs, belays, and pitches. When they look at the climb, they decide which gear should be conserved for higher in the pitch and which gear should be unloaded down low. They keep in mind that the team must climb fast at 6 AM to avoid deadly afternoon lightening storms. Deliberate thought allows climbers to create and enhance their safety envelope by anticipating hazards.

When you set out to master deliberate thought, it may appear to detract from the joy of climbing. In fact, deliberate thought can make climbing more enjoyable by providing a higher level of control. Besides, if you are unsafe, you won't have fun for long.

❖ Just Say No

One of the tenets of industrial safety is that every worker has the power to stop the work process. If you are the one who feels unsafe, stop whatever it is you are doing, review the circumstances, and upgrade the safety to an acceptable level.

If that is not possible, escape. Except under the worst circumstances, when your admission could unnerve your partner and cause more harm than good, admit when conditions scare you and fix the conditions.

❖ Attention to Detail
Climbing safety is a detail-oriented pursuit. To be safe, you must ferret out the details of rock quality, gear placement, tie-ins, fall distance, and so on. Inattention to detail leads to accidents. Some are born to detail attentiveness, some inherit detail attentiveness, and some achieve detail attentiveness. Either way, you will need this character trait to survive as a climber.

❖ Intuition
Some climbers successfully anticipate: route direction in the face of confusion, unseen bad rock, developing bad weather, and bad-luck days. If you believe that it is possible to develop intuition, you may do so by relying on "hunches" when they pertain to safety and seeing if your "hunches" pan out.

If the "hunches" lead to a higher peril than the evident danger, abide by the evident danger, keeping your intuition in check.

❖ Judgment
Good judgment, rather, is the ability to weigh facts, perceptions, and intuition to arrive at a favorable decision. If you do not have good judgment when you start climbing, the rigors of climbing can help you develop good judgment. Be open to what the rock, the environment, and others commu-

nicate; collect and organize your thoughts; developed reasoned plans; and learn from both good and bad outcomes.

YOUR PARTNER

Locating and Selecting Potential Partners

Locating a new partner is as difficult as finding a soul mate. Here are some of the ways to find partners and some of the pitfalls:

- Partner boards on the Internet or at climbing stores
- Through a friend
- Through a climbing gym
- On the crags

The first step in screening a partner is to talk to them at length. Face-to-face conversation provides the best screen. You should ask about their climbing experience, where they climb, where they learned, and what climbs they aspire to do. Sneak in questions about their attitude toward helmets and safety measures. Ask if the person likes to solo. Ask what training they have received. Have you ever been in an accident? What happened? Who do you usually climb with? What happened to them?

If you learn to intersperse these question with casual patter, you can avoid sounding like an interrogator. If the prospect has a broken hand and says he is still mourning his last partner ...well, you get the picture.

A person may be fundamentally safe, but if their ability and goals are vastly different than yours, this incompatibility itself could cause safety problems. If you are accustomed to

5.7 faces, and your partner drags you out on a 5.11 offwidth, you may be too nervous to be safe.

For the first time out, choose a familiar climb. If things go well, continue to develop your climbing partnership. Hold onto your reliable partners—climbing with the same people can enhance your safety margin because you develop and maintain good habits together. These habits will help you stay out of and escape trouble.

Photo 25. Having reliable partners enhances safety. Two doctors complete a safe day at Tunnel 2, Clear Creek, Colo.

Communicating With Partners

Once you find someone you like to climb with, be clear about your expectations and goals. Get around to discussing

107

things like who pays for what in the event expensive gear is lost and what your standards of comfort are on road trips. Although money, gear, and accommodations conflict seem remote from safety issues, the absence of goodwill can in fact undermine the safety of a team.

For on-the-rock communication, see the Climbing Safety Chapter.

Looking After Partners

You have a duty to safeguard your partner. Tell her if it looks like her hand is on a loose rock or if her foot is about to slip. Inspect his tie-in to make sure he is still secure. Tell her if her hex is about to fall out.

Few things are as disturbing as involvement in an accident or death with your partner. In the event of an accident, forget about the loss of gear and time or about any embarrassment or culpability you have. Your responsibility is to keep yourself safe and to safeguard your partner. See the Climbing Safety Chapter for technical details on climbing rescues.

Rock climbing in *Larger Groups* is unsafe for novices. Climbing in parties of three or more adds to the rope and anchor management duties and creates confusion. The only time climbing in larger groups enhances your safety is on expeditions or in certain big wall circumstances with expert teams.

OTHERS

Other climbers pose serious safety hazards:
- They can drop gear on you.
- They may fall on you or your partner.

- ❏ They can knock off rocks.
- ❏ They can cause avalanches.
- ❏ They can distract you.
- ❏ They can hog anchors forcing you onto a substandard anchor.
- ❏ They may steal fixed gear that is necessary for a careful ascent.
- ❏ Their dogs or other wards may distract or harm you.
- ❏ They may fail to render critical aid or share an emergency bivy.

Not only do other climbers pose a hazard to you, but they also endanger themselves. One of the most difficult duties in climbing is our duty to inform others when they are in danger. Few climbers enjoy intruding into other people "personal space." Clearly, if you feel an obligation to help someone who is hurt, you have the same obligation to help someone who is unaware of his or her exposure to a hazard.

The hard part is how do you tell someone that they are mistaken? Be friendly. Ask them if they would mind you sharing a safety tip with them. If they are open-minded, politely describe the hazard. If they gruffly tell you to keep to yourself, there is no need to be confrontational — they declined your offer.

An even more difficult responsibility arises when you see someone who is impaired by drugs or alcohol or who is sick. These people are unlikely to take up your offer of help. Nonetheless, you may wish to put on your best face and offer to help them.

Non-climbers do matter! They knock down rocks, pull guns, make drunken threats, steal packs, and distract belayers.

Other Cultures

People from different countries have different customs. Your unfamiliarity with them may cause confusion and compromise your safety. For example, some Europeans like to simul-rappel—a technique where partners rappel at the same time on opposite strands of rope. An unpracticed miscue with this technique could be fatal.

Guides

Nobody is perfect. There have been incidents where guides have perished in crevasses while guiding. There was a well-known case involving a client who fell out of his harness while being guided. If you need no other example, consider the clients who died with their guides while climbing Mt. Everest in the fatal 1996 season.

Do not believe that anyone can watch every move of two or more clients all of the time. When with a guide, learn to think for yourself, and don't be afraid to ask pointed questions. If you want to see how a circumspect client should act, read Jon Krakauer's, *Into Thin Air*, and focus on how he behaved.

Boyfriends/Girlfriends/Spouses

Some of the most dangerous mismatches in climbing have been highly competitive men with less capable women. In a couple of cases, the men have failed to safeguard their significant others, resulting in the women's death.

Wizard Tip—Attachment or obligations to others may cloud your ability to climb as safely as possible. You may be so preoccupied with the comfort or goodwill of another that your safety margin slips. Heighten your attention to safety when with people you care about.

One scenario involves the boyfriend/girlfriend in retreat. On the retreat, the man decides that they can escape unroped. The woman takes a fatal fall while soloing.

If someone feels unsafe, then he or she must insist on the necessary safety measures. If you continuously feel unsafe, follow your intuition and find a different partner.

Children

People increasingly bring their whole families to the crags. Rock or gear fall is much more hazardous to children than it is to adults. Children cannot anticipate falling stuff; they are more likely than adults to fall on third-class terrain, and their developing bodies are more prone to serious injury. "All in the Family" is especially dangerous at popular crags.

Cliff edges are particularly hazardous to children because many children lack sufficient fear of falling, and consequently, are not cautious enough at cliff edges.

Property Owners

Trespassing climbers have been shot at and threatened by unwelcoming property owners. Beware if you climb without permission.

*Safety in rock climbing lies almost entirely with...
judgment... Little is left to chance. Equipment is
a minor factor. With the best equipment in the
world the man with poor judgment is in mortal
danger.*
Royal Robbins

SUMMARY

There is no way to safeguard against all rock-climbing risks.
Even so, climbers can adopt equipment, methods of preparation, climbing methods, personal conduct, and styles of
interacting with others that reduce the risk:

- ❏ First and foremost, acknowledge that each and
  every climber has the greatest control over his
  or her own risk.
- ❏ Adopt a *safety culture*—let the management of
  risk be the overriding consideration that per-
  meates your climbing.
- ❏ Choose your partners carefully. A safe and
  competent partner can make up for your own
  lack of foresight, equipment, and knowledge.
  An unsafe, incompetent partner creates risk
  where little existed and can cause serious injury or death.
- ❏ Prepare yourself for each and every climb. Be
  mindful of the tendency to ignore familiar risks
  and the risks at familiar areas.
- ❏ When climbing, name all hazards, especially
  fall hazards, to yourself. Hazard identification
  is the starting point to risk management.

- Anchors and tie-ins are the centerpieces of climbing safety. Evaluate each and every one. Learn to identify a minimally sufficient anchor and avoid using substandard anchors at all costs.
- Check and re-check your tie-in and those of others throughout the climbing day.
- Back-up fixed gear at every opportunity.
- Learn to create "nut clusters" or "nut strings" that re-establish your rope chain to the rock as you progress.
- Carry and use nuts and cams on sport climbs.
- Be cautious on approaches and descents.
- Reduce or block out distractions. A moment's distraction can precipitate an accident.
- Check and re-check each and every element of rappels.
- Develop safe habits and routines. In an emergency, you will fall back on your habits, and sound habits can carry you through hardship.

APPENDIX A

Health Considerations

Accidental injury and death come to mind when climbers think of the adverse consequences inherent in climbing. In the short term, those are the serious concerns, but climbing can also lead to long-term adverse health consequences. Climbers should be aware of these:

- ❑ Climbing over long periods, especially intense climbing and training, can lead to musculoskeletal disorders (MSDs). MSDs include tendonitis, arthritis, carpal tunnel and tarsal tunnel syndrome (inflammation of the wrist and hand or foot, respectively). All of these cumulative disorders can be disabling and prevent climbers from climbing and from doing even everyday activities. If you wish to avoid MSDs, avoid climbing too much, over-training, and exercising injured body parts. Remember, pain is your body's way of telling you to take a break.

- ❑ Sun exposure causes skin cancer. Don't ignore the need to cover-up, use sunscreen, and avoid the mid-day sun. Lips are especially vulnerable, and their exposure is often ignored by outdoor sports people.

- ❑ Traumatic injury, such as broken bones, can lead to arthritis later in life. Avoid breaking bones.

- ❑ Single head injuries, and even multiple, low-impact head injuries have been linked to neurological diseases such as Alzheimer's disease. Diligently avoid all head injury.

- Chronic dehydration is bad for your kidneys. Don't make "gutting-it-out" — going without water — a lifelong habit; this could contribute to later kidney disease.
- If you are one of the few and the mighty who put up bolt routes for a living, be aware of the long-term health effects of exposure to noise and silica dust. Noise exposure causes hearing loss, and fine-grained silica dust can cause silicosis, a deadly disease with no cure. Note, whereas drilling granite, quartzite and sandstone produce deadly silica dust, limestone dust is not known to be a health hazard.
- Rodent feces can transmit disease like the deadly hanta virus. Try to avoid touching or breathing rodent waste and dust. This material occurs on ledges as moist-brown balls, dry, dusty clots and in nests.
- One or many "hard landings" due to bouldering falls or accidental ground falls can contribute to later arthritis or cause immediate nerve compressing. Compressed nerves may cause you to lose sensation on your lower body. Use "crash pads" when hard landings are likely.
- Climbing has always attracted more than its share of the emotionally dysfunctional. Don't let climbing become your crutch for avoiding the job of everyday life. If you have an emotional disorder, don't lapse into the climbing lifestyle as a refuge from your emotional problems. Climbing is a traditional refuge for unhappiness, and drug and alcohol abuse. Be

kindly, counsel those who are dysfunctional into getting help. Being a good person is more important than being a great climber.

APPENDIX B

Annotated Bibliography and References

American Safe Climbing Association, <http://www.safeclimbing.org>. (Non-profit devoted to safe climbing. Website has extensive collection of technical information.)

Dill, John, 1999, "Staying Alive," 22 p. <http://www.bluebison.net/yosar/alive.htm>. (Overview of climbing safety with emphasis on Yosemite Valley issues.)

Ditmer, Joanne, 06-12-2001, "Outdoor Fun Still No. 1," The Denver Post, Colo., Section F, p. 1 and 2. (References number of climbers.)

Long, John, 1998, *How To Rock Climb:* Chockstone Press, Helena, Montana, 208 p. (Definitive discussion of all aspects of basic rock climbing; extensive safety information throughout the text.)

Long, John, 1999, *Climbing Anchors:* Falcon Press, Helena, Mont., 112 p. (Detailed descriptions of anchor construction, evaluation and use.)

Raleigh, Duane, 2001, "Mechanical Bolts," American Safe Climbing Association, 11 p. <http://www.safeclimbing.org/bolt_types.html>. (Detailed discussion of bolts.)

Storrick, Gary, 1995, "My Internet Post on Rappel Safeties, 4 p. <http://storrick.cnhost.com/VerticalDevicesPage/Misc/RappelSafetyPost.html>. (Good discussion of risks posed by use of rappel back-ups/safeties.)

Suber, Peter, 2001, "Knots on the Web," 36 p. <http://www.earlham.edu/~peters/knotlink.htm>. (Exhaustive directory of knots—books, videos, websites.)

Weare, Damian, 1997, "Technical Advice—Rope Life," <http://www.hoefo.de/srt/srt_english.htm>. (Details about rope life and cave techniques.)

Williamson, Jed, ed., 2000, "Accidents in North American Mountaineering," American Alpine Club, Golden, Colo., v. 7, no. 5, issue 53, 90 p. (Essential safety reading.)

Ultrasafe

INDEX

W

NOTES

NOTES

NOTES

Order Form

ULTRASAFE—A Guide to Safer Rock Climbing

Your name: _____

Address: _____

_____

_____

Email: _____

Phone: _____

Quantity of books ordered: _____

Total cost of books ordered: $_____
(one copy = $13.95, two or more
copies = $13.00 each)

Shipping and Handling: $_____
(one copy, add $2; two or more copies, add
$1.50 each; Priority Mail, add $5 per book)
Add 3.2% tax for all books shipped to a Colorado address.

Total enclosed: $_____

Please pay by Check or Money Order.
Allow 30 days for delivery; 10 days for Priority Mail.

Remit to: PP Preventive Press LLC
            2343 W. Hyacinth Rd.
            Highlands Ranch, CO 80129

Your book(s) will be promptly sent upon receipt of payment.

ACCESS: IT'S EVERY CLIMBER'S CONCERN

The Access Fund, a national, non-profit climbers organization, works to keep climbing areas open and to conserve the climbing environment.

Climbers can help preserve access by being committed to leaving the environment in its natural state. Here are some simple guidelines:

•ASPIRE TO CLIMB WITHOUT LEAVING A TRACE, especially in environmentally sensitive areas like caves. Pick up litter, and leave trees and plants intact.

•DISPOSE OF HUMAN WASTE PROPERLY Use toilets whenever possible. If toilets are not available, dig a "cat hole" at least six inches deep and 200 feet from any water, trails, campsites, or the base of climbs. *Always pack out toilet paper.* On big wall routes, use a "poop tube" and carry waste up and off with you (the old "bag toss" is now illegal in many areas).

•USE EXISTING TRAILS Cutting switchbacks causes erosion. When walking off-trail, tread lightly, especially in the desert. Be aware that "rim ecologies" (the clifftop) are often highly sensitive to disturbance.

•BE DISCRETE WITH FIXED ANCHORS *Bolts are controversial and are not a convenience—don't place them unless they are really necessary.* Camouflage all anchors. Remove unsightly slings from rappel stations (better to use steel chain or welded cold shuts).

•RESPECT THE RULES and speak up when other climbers don't. Expect restrictions in designated wilderness areas, rock art sites, caves, and to protect wildlife, especially nesting birds of prey. *Power drills are illegal in Wilderness and all national parks.*

•PARK AND CAMP IN DESIGNATED AREAS Some climbing areas require a permit for overnight camping.

•MAINTAIN A LOW PROFILE Leave the boom box and day-glo clothing at home—the less climbers are heard and seen, the better.

•RESPECT PRIVATE PROPERTY Be courteous to land owners. Don't climb where you're not wanted.

•JOIN THE ACCESS FUND To become a member, make a tax-deductible donation of $25.

THE ACCESS FUND
Keeping climbing areas open and conserving the climbing environment
PO Box 17010
Boulder, CO 80308
303.545.6772 • www.accessfund.org